Value Profiles of School Students

Value Profiles of School Students

By

Dr. R.K. Patro
Lecturer in Education
Chikiti Mahavidyalaya
District–Ganjam (Orissa)
India

&

Dr. B.C. Mishra
M.Phil., Ph.D., D.D.E., P.G.D.H.E.
Senior Lecturer in Education
D.P.I.A.S.E., Berhampur
Ganjam, (Orissa)
India

DISCOVERY PUBLISHING HOUSE
NEW DELHI-110002

First Published-2007
Reprinted: 2013
ISBN 81-7141-726-4

Published by
DISCOVERY PUBLISHING HOUSE
4831/24, Ansari Road, Prahlad Street,
Darya Ganj, New Delhi-110002 (India)
Phone: 23279245 • Fax: 91-11-23253475
E-mail:dphtemp@indiatimes.com

Printed at: Dynamic printers, Delhi

PREFACE

The question of values has been exercising the minds of thinkers around the world including our own country for the last many years. They feel the need of a new value pattern for reconstructing the human community. The need is no less in our own country. In fact if the idea that India faces any severe danger of self-amalitation, it is the one that emanates from the character of its present value pattern. As the NPE (1986) states: The growing concern over the erosion of essential values and an increasing cynicism in society has brought to focus the need for readjustments in the curriculum in order to make education a forceful tool for the cultivation of social and moral values.

The development of values and moral character is a recurring theme in the recommendations of major committees and commissions on education. Value system plays an important role in the decision-making process. In fact, every human action is the reflection of personal or social values. The present situation of India calls for a system of education which apart from strengthening national unity must strengthen social solidarity through meaningful and constructive value education. Before launching any comprehensive educational programme to promote students' values, it is essential to know the prevalent value systems held by the students.

The present work is an attempt to study the value profiles of attempt to study the value profiles of students across their stream, residential background, sex and achievement level and further to compare different groups with respect to their values.

The findings of the study are quite revealing and interesting. It is hoped that these findings will help the teachers, educational planners and administrators in different ways.

The authors would like to appreciate the cooperation of the heads of the sample institutions and teachers while collecting data.

We are also grateful to the sample students for their kind cooperation and valuable responses.

Thanks are due to the U.G.C, authority for the financial support in conducting the present piece of work.

Lastly, we gratefully acknowledges the excellent work of Discovery Publishing House, the wholehearted cooperation extended by Mr. Tilak Wasan, the Proprietor and his able assistants in bringing out the book in record time.

Rajesh Kumar Patro
Brundaban Chandra Mishra

CONTENTS

1
CONCEPTUAL ANALYSIS OF VALUES

Among all the living, human life is the most evolved creation in the universe. The excellence or superiority of human life as compared to other living beings can be easily identified. A man's life has to possess some meaning beyond mere self-preservation or existence. In case of other creatures their life is manipulated by man in his own interest. Man is the only such unique creation in this universe who is under certain parameters free to make his own destiny.

Mankind has travelled a long way from a 'nomadic' to 'pastoral'; from a 'pastoral' to an 'agricultural'; from an 'agricultural' to an 'industrial'; and from an 'industrial' to a postindustrial civilization and now to a nuclear age. Our present age is witnessing sweeping technological changes. Startling strides of development have been registered in different field of science and the crux of the problem is that human spirit has been far outstripped by fantastic changes which have caused chaos and confusion and the loss of moorings and directions. The dignity and value of the individual person is threatened by the brute force and insensate behaviour of the faceless. Mass of machine and the totalitarian compulsions of society. There is such a widespread spectrum of sensuality and deceit, dissension and conflict. Jealousy and hatred, sycophancy and hypocrisy, bribery and corruption that this world has indeed become too unbearable to live in serious citizens of the rising generations feel lost in a mass of contradictions and complexities. They are nonplussed when they witness greedy politicians, treachorous demagogues, unscrupulous, business barons wily self-seekers, downright drunkards, brazen drug-pushers and moral wrecks are not merely tolerated but even honoured as paragons of virtue. Then again, they are deeply perturbed by the outbursts of narrow sectarianism, unashamed regionalism and outrageous fanaticism. Reality is seen by them to be at variance with the values taught by teachers and text-books. They are quite disturbed by the existing dichotomy between profession and practice, promise and performance. They have a feeling that values are cunningly women myth to lull them into silence or take them for a ride. Rampant corruption has been playing the devil with the life of the common man. Reason has taken the backseat and emotions have been running riot.

A distinguished scientist, Prof. D.S. Kothari, who headed the Education Commission (1964-66) has thus described the grave aberrations afflicting our world "knowledge is expanding but human personality is shrinking". On the one hand we have the exponentially rising, growing spiral of science, technology and productivity, the STP spiral, and on the other we have greed, hatred and delusion, the GHD spiral. If we are to prevent further defacement and defilement of our culture, the foundations of a refurbished value system must be strongly laid in the minds and hearts of the people as urged by the constitution of UNESCO. The material power of man which springs from the dominance of science and technology needs to be bridled and tempered by the pursuit of a quality of life based on the faith in and sincere practice of human values. The concept of quality of life says Dr. Prem Kripal, an eminent educationist, is an emerging vision of our items, sometimes reflected in the spirit and attitudes of idealistic youth. A pointed out by him, "the humanism of the past was based upon man's discovery of himself followed by liberation from taboos and dogmas imposed by fear. Superstition and unreasons; the human of tomorrow seeks to substitute love of power, stresses the brotherhood of man and his common humanity and probes towards a new relationship for man with his conmos a new humanism free wise compassionate and loving and ever aspiring to the light on the hills and the stars beyond."

Today, thus is both a striving and search for a sound philosophy that can sustain the human race in this nuclear age. For this purpose education can aid us. Education helps us in acquiring knowledge. Information needs to be digested to become knowledge and knowledge should nature in to wisdom Prof. A.N. Whitehead that "Unapplied knowledge is knowledge shorn of its meaningful and fruitful should help one to live a "full-life" "to drink the cup of life to the less" as Tennysons ulysses would say and it should be a continuous and life long affairs.

THE CONCEPT OF VALUE

It is not a very easy task to define 'value' satisfactorily. Some philosophers have even considered it as a fundamental category, as indefinable like 'yellow' yet the concept of value is so deeply embedded in human actions and thoughts that one should make an effort at least one should make an effort at least to understand its meaning and ramifications.

Values refer to objects that we people cherish and desire and consider them desirable and worthy of acquisition. These may include material objects like food, clothing and shelter etc, and abstract qualities and ideas like truth, beauty, goodness, happiness, peace, punctuality, justice etc. Thus a thing has a value if it has 'worthiness to be chosen'. In the words of Dewey (1966) "to value means primarily to prize to esteem to appraise, to estimate. It means the act of cherishing something, holding it dear and also the act of passing judgement upon the nature and amount of its value as compared with something else". Perry (1950) defines value "as the relation of an object to a valuing subject". If the art of valuing means liking, desiring, then value is any object of any interest. Lindzay (1964) defines "values" as "a person's idea of what is desirable, what he and others want not necessarily what he actually wants" Kluckhohn (1957) defined "value as a conception, explicit or implicit, distinctive of an individual or characteristic of a group of these desirable or characteristic of a group of these desirable which influences the selection from available modes, and ends of action". Rokeach (1973) viewed value as an enduring belief, a specific mode of conduct or end state of existence along a continuum of relative importance. Any conception of human values if it is to be fruitful, it must be able to account for the enduring character of values as well as their changing character. The enduring character of values arises mainly by their initial teaching and learning in isolation from other values. A mode of behaviour or end state is always desirable. The isolated and absolute learning of values more or less guarantees their endurance and stability. In case of values as a belief, Rokeach (1968) has distinguished three types of beliefs: (I) descriptive or existential beliefs, something being true or false; (II) evaluative beliefs wherein the object of belief is judged to be good or bad; and (III) prescriptive or proscriptive beliefs, where in some means or end of action is judged to be desirable or undesirable. Values like all beliefs have congnitive, affective and behavioural components. A value refers to a mode of conduct or end state of existence.

A value is a preference as well as the conception of the preferable. According to Kluchohn (1957) a value is a "conception of the desirable" and not something "merely desired". A conception of the desirable appears to be nothing more than a special kind of preference- a preferece for one mode of behaviour over an opposite mode, or a preference for one end state over other end state. Thus, a value is a conception of something that is personally or socially preferable. When a person speaks about his values, it can't be assumed that he necessarily intends to apply them differently to young or old, men or women, rich or poor and so on.

Values, in the words of Shaver (1962) are "standards and principles for judging worth. They are criteria by which we judge things (people, objects, ideas, actions and situations) to be good, worthwhile despicable, or of course, somewhere in between these extremes. We may apply our values consciously or they may function unconsciously as a part of the influence of our frame of reference, without our being aware of the standards implied by our decisions". The definitions of Shaver (1962) includes three key elements:

(I) The values are concepts, not feelings. Values embody and express feelings, but they are more than feelings. They are standards for judgement with rational content. Because of the rational content, a given value can be defined, analysed and compared with other values. A value is a concept that carries criteria for rating the things. Thus a value holds affect, but its defining structure is cognitive.

(II) Values exist in the mind independently of self awareness or public affirmation. A value does not have to be explicitly announced or put into practice to quality as a value. Values often form a part of frame of judgement without man's conscious knowledge or deliberate choosing.

(III) Values are dimensional rather than absolute categories. In other words they are criteria for judging degrees of good and bad, right or worng, or praise or blame. Values are not simply the presence or absence of these characteristics. They are sets of rules for rating behaviours or objects along a continuum of worth (Hersh, Miller and Fielding, 1980).

For Shaver (1962) there is difference between values and value judgements. Value judgements are the assertions an individual used to make on the basis of his/her values. Thus values are grounds not conclusions. Values are constructs that underline value judgements, not judgement per so. The value judgements and values may be related to each other. To justify the appropriateness and property of value judgements the values should be consulted on which value judgements are based. Values should be understood as interlocking parts of a total value system rather than self-contained units, because human values are linked to one another, one value often impinges on another value.

Values are thus standards that group members share, by which they judge whether an action or even an object is beautiful, good, right or lawful. Values originate in the socio-cultural milieu of a given social system and are thus governed by the standards that each social system sets for itself. Owing to this reason that values of one social group differs from that of another. Differing values represent key aspects of variations in human culture. Thus one's value is strongly influenced by the specific culture in which they happen to live.

Values are closely related to norms. But in a broader sense values can be differentiated from norms. The term 'norm' could be used for a relatively specific pattern of expected behaviour. A norm sets certain limits for behaviour. Since norms are backed by group pressures, their violation generally calls for negative sanctions.

On the other hand, value is a matter of one's choice. Both values and norms are internalised by group members in the process of learning called 'socialisation'. It determines one's appreciation, acceptance, and adoption of type of value of norm. Development of values is thus an intrinsic part of the socialisation process. Values are crucial to any society because they serve as criteria for selection of action. Values also act as the base for judgement, preference, choice or rejection. Different cultures have different value systems and these value systems are conditioned by the developments taking place in a cultural set-up.

CLASSIFICATION OF VALUES

Values having been defined as something that is justifiably favoured or desired, classification of values naturally follows from the universe of justified desires or interests. Justifiability includes positiveness, because positiveness of desire or of interest itself serves as a factor in favour of the desire or interest being justified. According to Iyengar (1942), "The classification of values will naturally depend on our classification of the dominant universe of desire in man".

Classification of values into higher and lower is perhaps recognised by all schools of philosophy except the carvakas or India materialists and some counterparts elsewhere. But it can be stated that the first axiom of the philosophy of value is that certain things or acts are preferable to or worthier than others, otherwise there can be no question of choosing values. We can come to the concept of higher and lower values by comparing an animal with a man. Man is a rational animal due to his reflective consciousness. It is special in man and all other things such as hunger, sleep, fear, sex etc, are common to animals and men. Thus reflective conscious is regarded as a higher value as compared to all those like pleasure, sleep, sex etc.

The upanisad differentiates man from animals for his 'self-consciousness' which gives the capacity for self-criticism. Self-criticism needs a standard by which one criticises oneself, one's wants or state of being. This concepts of a standard is never ending because one standard, in order to be justified requires another higher standard and so on till the highest standard is reached.

Classification of values is also made on the basis of theory of reality. Materialists like carvakas to whom reality constitutes only of matter, even mind being an effect of matter-there are only two kinds of values 'Kama' and 'artha' in English terminology intrinsic and instrumental values respectively. There is an ontological explanation of man's being. Man is constituted of five 'Kosas' or sheaths. They are 'Annamayakosa'; 'Pranamayakosa'; 'manonmayakosa' 'Vijnanamayakosaand' 'anandamayakosa' respectively refering to the physical, physiological, psychological, intellectual and spiritual aspects.

As the 'Kosas' are said to be hierarchical 'annamayakosa' being the lowest and 'anandamayakosa' being the higest, the values or things and activities that cater to them are also in a hierarchy. The lower values being 'artha' and 'kama'; and the higher ones 'dharma' and 'moksa' 'Artha' and 'dharma' are recognised as instrumental values; 'kama' and 'moksa' as intrinsic values. Again 'artha' and 'kama' are regarded as basic, secular as well as lower values whereas 'dharma' and 'moksa' are regarded as higher as well as spiritual.

The Modern Classification of Values

The modern philosophers like Brightman (1940), Perry (1954) Broudy (1965) and Iyengar (1965) have given the following classes of values :

(i) **Organic or Health Value**—This class of values arise out of man's desire for self-sustenance, self-preservation etc, and include food, drink, cloth, health, strength and in adult life, sex. They are also called primary or basic values, as self-sustenance and self-preservation etc. Primarily depend upon them.

(ii) **Hedonic or Pleasure Values**—Man desires pleasure, satisfaction, happiness and well-being etc. Although there can be difference as regards comprehensiveness and duration, in essence they are similar. Thus they can be grouped under the common concept of hedonic or pleasure value.

(iii) **Recreational Values**—Man's desire and involvement in different kinds of play and recreation is so dominant that although they are known for values of pleasure, health etc, are now recognised as a distnict class of values.

(iv) **Aesthetic Values**—There is in man a sense of beauty which seems to have existed from the very beginning of mankind. Man sees beauty in nature as well as in things he creates. Natural beauty gives spontaneous joy and feeling of wonder. But when man creats beauty in art, music, drama, dance, poetry etc, besides giving joy to others, he also gets the joy of self-expression in elegant forms. Thus all those things and activities which give joys of beauty come under aesthetic values.

(v) **Economic Values**—The objects that command a money price are said to have economic value. In a broader sense, all that have an exchange value may be said to have an economic value. It is in this sense that the economic values prevailed in barter system even before the concept of money was born. Economic values are known as instrumental values because they are not valued for themselves but for the enjoyments the make possible.

(vi) **Personal Values**—These are the values which a person desires or cherishes as his own. They include his joys, ambitions, personal, possessions and pursuits. It is supposed that in cherishing and possessing these values he does not affect others.

(vii) **Social Values**—These are the values which are made possible because of association with others friendship, love, membership with institutions are instances of social values. Other values such as economic, aesthetic etc, can also be considered as social if they are possessed or desired jointly by a social group.

Then it can be seen that personal and social values are correlated and all other values can be subsumed under them depending upon the consideration as to how far they are personal or social.

(viii) **Intellectual Value**—Man desires to know truth in any of its forms. Although knowledge of truth is made use of in various ways, truth itself gives satisfaction. Thus all those things or activities which help finding truth through intelluctual understanding can be looked upon as having intellectual value.

(ix) **Moral Values**—Morality, Peters (1981) says, "then is concerned with what there are reasons for doing or not doing, for bringing into or removing from existence". He further adds "..........principles are needed to determine the relevance of reasons and that some principles seem more justifiable than others". Moral values are the satisfactions or dissatisfactions that accrue to the individual in the course of his attempts to make right choices (Broudy, 1965). Aristotle *et al.*n (1898) writes "while we wish for the end, we deliberate upon and choose the means there to. Actions that are concerned with means, then will be guided by choice, and so will be voluntary". But the acts in which the virtues are manifested are concerned with means (Aristotle *et at,* 1898). Thus any conception or theory of morality, if it has to be meaningful or justifiable, has to be linked with some kind of conception which is purely philosophical, religious or spiritual. That is why Bhyrappa (1968) is of the view: "a moral notion that rufuses to recognise its own roots remains vapoury". He further adds "unless morality matures into spiritual perfection it can not get its fullest justification".

(x) **Spiritual Values**—Man is not a gross body. There is a power beyond this matter which governs it. That is spirit. Man is a spiritual being. He is a spark of the divine. Spirituality is his essence. It is very difficult to define spirit.

Radhakrishnan (1947) writes: "we know it, but we cannot explain it. It is felt everywhere though seen nowhere. It is not the physical body or the vital organism, the mind or the will, but something which underlies them all and sustain them. It is the basis and background of our being, the universality that cannot be reduced to this or that formula".

The highest spiritual state cannot be thought of as something remaining outside of man. The kingdom of heaven is within you. One's original state or reality is revealed by means of self-control, self-purification and cultivation of virtues.

When one progresses in spiritual life, one becomes enlightened, wise, contented, peaceful and joyous. The spirituality and spiritual values need not be thought of as something alien to man. Every knowledge, every act, every feeling that leads one higher and higher in the value hierarchy become steps in the spiritual ladder. One, who, keeping the highest spiritual goal in view integrates his values becomes consciously spiritual, ensuring a steady and unceasing progress.

THEORIES OF VALUES

Theories of values have been developed to understand the nature and status of values and the more of substantive issues too. In this sense, theories of values are many which can broadly be grouped under two categories : (i) normative and (ii) meta-normative theories. Normative theories deal with the questions: 'what is good ?' or 'what has valuest ?' 'what is bad ?' etc. On the other hand, metanormative theories analyse 'good', 'value' etc, and try to show the meaning or use of these terms. Thus they show how a value judgement is made and whether justification can be given for value judgement and normative theories.

Metanormative Theories of Values

The cognitivists in value theory assert that terms like 'value' and 'good' stand for properties of objects or kind of objects. The naturalistic cognitivists view that property involved is a natural or empirical one which can be defined. Aristotle and Perry etc., hold that value is a relation property of being an object of desire or interest. Lewis and Rice claim that value is the quality of being, enjoyed or enjoyable in some way. It is an affective theory of value.

To Hiriyanna (1975) value is "that which is desired". This makes him a normativist.

Some other philisophers assert that goodness or value is an indefinable non-natural quality. They are intuitionists or non-naturalists. To them value belongs to objects independently whether one desires, enjoys or values them.

The analytical philosophers and existentialists are of the opinion that value terms do not stand for properties and that judgement of value is not property ascribing. Therefore, they are called non cognitivists or anti-descriptivists.

Broadly metanormative theories include naturalistic, intuitive and emotive theories of value which are discussed below.

Naturalistic Theories of Value

The naturalists vary in their conception of value. Some view that values are properties that inhere in objects. The properties of objects are not alone responsible for value. The same object is not valued by all.

Some other naturalists believe that the seat of value is in the nature of man. But it is quite difficult to determine the true nature of man. Empirical evidences about man's nature give conflicting conclusions.

Some are selfish, some are rational and still some are pleasure seeking and so on. Further more the same man can behave differently at different times. Which nature of man is to be developed ? Again man may be found to be some particular nature, but how can 'man is' converted to man ought to be.

Man has not remained the same as he was thousands of years ago. Why then his present state or present nature be prepetuated? The psychological theories which explain what man's nature generally is, therefore fail to have a philosophical appeal in the form of what man ought to be.

Intuitive Theories of Value

Like naturalists the intuitionists agree that values are objective. The intuitionists claim that terms like 'good' and 'ought' etc. do not stand for observable qualities or relations. Thus value inferences are not from any form of empirical generalizations. The intuitionism takes different forms. Moore (1903) believes that good refers to a simple non-natural, unanalysable property like 'yellow' which can't be sensed but intuited. But if what is good is apprehended directly, why is there so much argument about what is good ? Why all people do not apprehend same thing as good ?

Differences may be seen in intuitions. Intuition may be fallible. Again there is the difficulty of making others agree what one holds to be intuitively good or valuable. Thus intuitionism which holds some sort of 'objectivity' lands itself in relativity or Subjectivity. But the arguments of intuitionists that all types of knowledge are not empirical and logical, and that intuition is also a type of knowledge, is very strong. Again intuitionism advocates a strong poing that reasoning is value judgement is very different in respect of its justification from reasoning about what is, was or will be the case. It preserves autonomy of values. The intuitionists hold that certain values, particularly the highest value or ultimate reality can be realised intuitively alone.

Emotive Theories of Value

Some philosophers are of the opinion that no rational justification of value is possible and that arbitrariness must be in the nature of values judgements. They compare value judgements to judgements of expressions of tastes or commands based on emotions. The emotivists contend that owrds do not stand for properties, They speak of, they have rather emotive meanings. Thus the meaning of 'good' and 'ought' was also thought of in similar way. Ayer (1946) and

Stevenson (1944) developed sophisticated versions of this approach to ethical and value terms like 'good'. This is good was analysed by Stevenson (1944) as I approve of this do so as well. This analysis deprives 'good' of any objectivity and justifiability and renders it as an expression of emotion and/or command. But every word does not have an emotive meaning. Again a word may be conveying emotional feeling, but there may be something that arouses emotions. The emotive theories of value attempt to explicate value judgement in terms of emotions, attitudes or feelings of approval and disapproval. But how can these be caused without the appraisal of something as being right or wrong?

The emotive theories preserve autonomy of value, but it is done at the cost of objectivity. They are subjectivists. The view that a person bestows value on some objective, can not be maintained wholly. Thus basing value judgements on emotions, feelings, attitudes etc., and considering values as totally subjective or relative does not give an adequate explanation. However, these theories have made a significant contribution by linking value judgement with feeling.

Normative Theories of Value

Normative theories of value are primarily concerned with the question 'what' kinds of things are good? and 'what' kinds of actions should one perform? or what has intrinsic value which can be taken as the end of human pursuit. Some philosophers have answered that the 'good' or end is pleasure. They are called the hedonists. Hume, Bentham etc. among the Westerners and the charvakas among the Indians hold this kind of view. Some others hold a quasi-hedonistic view. For them, it is not pleasure, but very similar to it, such as happiness, satisfaction etc. Dewey, Lewis and Parker etc., belong to this category.

Hedonistic Theories of Value

The hedonists find so qualitative difference in different kinds of pleasure, therefore have no conception of values as higher or lower. But it is axiomatic in the philosophy of value that something is preferable to or worthier than others. No doubt pleasurable feeling may be the reason of thinking something valuable, but the fact that man prefers one kind of pleasure to that of others and also that he prefers comparatively more permanent pleasure to the pleasure that is momentary, reveals that the reason is not as simple as the hedonists think.

Again there are different ways of getting pleasure, without some kind of principle, pleasure seeking efforts of human beings will end in chaos. Thus the narrower view of value as pleasure, happiness etc, do not explain well of value.

Anti-hedonistic Theories of Value

Anti-hedonistic theories are of two types. Some agree that in the final analysis, there is only one thing that is good or good making but deny that it is pleasure. Yet different philosophers state it as different things. For instance, to Aristotle, it is audaemonia or excellent activity; to Augustine and Aquinas it is communication with God; to Spinoza, it is knowledge; to Bradley, it is self-realization; to Nietzche, it is power; to Hindus it is 'moksa', to Buddhists, it is 'Nirvana' etc. Thus no value can be justified ultimately without reference to a norm which should be nothing short of ultimate or absolute value. Hiriyana (1975) believes the necessity of a 'standard' which can be nothing short of absolute perfection. Therefore, adequate theory of value, can not but have to have a conception of ultimate value.

2

SOCIO-CULTURAL AND PSYCHOLOGICAL BASES OF VALUE DEVELOPMENT

In the course of our discussion we have touched the problem of values. Values, as we have seen, is an enduring belief that a specific mode of conduct of state of existence is personally or socially preferable to an opposite or converse mode of conduct or state of existence. Thus values are standards that group members share, by which they judge whether an action or even an object is beautiful, good, right and lawful. Values originate in the socio-cultural milieu of a given social system and are thus governed by the standards that each social system sets for itself. For this reason values of one social group differs from that of another. One's value system is profoundly influenced by the specific culture in which they happen to live.

Socialisation, the process of learning the dominant cultural patterns of a given social system is also the chief course of value development. Socialisation covers all the processes by which anyone-from infancy to old age-acquires his/her social skills, roles, norms, values and personality patterns. To put it in other way, socialisation results in what could be called internalisation of those values which are symbolic of a culture at a given point of time. Since time immemorial societies have followed the strategy of trying to get their members believe in and to accept inwardly those values which are felt to be pivotal to their survival and growth.

Now it can be said that development of values is an intrinsic part of the socialisation process. Values are basic to any society because they serve as criteria for selection of action. Values act as the base for judgement, preference, choice or rejection too. It is a fact that different cultures have different value systems which are conditioned by the developments taking place in a cultural context. Thus values have a strong social and cultural base.

Some values are positive and some are negative ones and they are decided by the culturally defined norms at a given point of time. For example in a culture set-up where discipline, courtesy etc. are considered most important, rude behaviour, lack of manners would be considered as negative values. On the other hand in a cultural context where violence, criminal instances are tolerated and approved, values which have been considered as negative, namely disrespect for laws, dishonesty receive social sanctions.

In this way, an individual's consideration of values as positive or negative is often determined primarily by the kind of upbringing he or she had. An individuals attitude is shaped by the socialisation process, which he or she has undergone, and that determines the choice of values. Thus, values are basically social in origin as well as in their manifestation. Values are considered as important and utilisation only in their social context. The more complex a society becomes, the greater is the need for the operation of values.

Now a question comes to our mind: How are values acquired? It is a fact that values are best absorbed by observation and by unconscious emulation of the ideas, ideals and actions of important men and women. Values manifest themselves in the process, how individuals behave in a given situation. In all critical situations when great and crucial issues are at stake, the ultimate line of action is decided mainly by the set of values which a given society upholds. The values that determine and direct our actions are acquired through a series of experiences which one undergoes in certain important social institutions.

The family is the first unit with which the child has continuous contact and it becomes the most powerful medium through which value systems develop. The family experts a sizeable influence on the growth of attitudes and interests of an individual. The power and influences of the family are well brought out by Macaiver and Page (1950) in the following words.

> ***Of all organisations, large or small, which society unfolds, none transcends the family in the intensity of its sociological significance. It influences the whole life of society in innumerable ways, and its changes, as we shall see, reverberate through the whole social structure. It is capable of endless variation and yet reveals a remarkable continuity and persistence through change.***

A child is born to a family and the family places him or her in a community, which is part of a particular society. All sub-cultures are based on different types of social differentiations of which, in the

Indian set-up, the caste system is of particular significance in the enculturation of some of the values. In an Indian family, the important determinants of authority which a person can weild are age, gender and generational status. Irrespective of personal talents or achievements, respect for traditions, deference to age and differential treatment on the basis of status are values which are often inculcated in the youngsters in the Indian family set-up. Thus, the family's capacity for both preventing or precipitating the cultivation of different types of values is very much there. Lessons learnt in the family can go a long way in the shaping of human personality. The family is the singlemost important channel through which values, considered conducive to individual and social good could be cultivated.

The concept of neighbourhood has both physical and social implications. Physically, it refers to a part of a town or a city or a district, with clear-cut boundaries. Socially, a neighbourhood is characterised by social similarities of the residents, often especially by similarity of social class or status and other identities.

The entire life of an individual is spent within the same neighbourhood. It is the neighbourhood that one is likely to come under influences, which may help or hinder the development of 'positive values'. Constant contact with the neighbourhood institutions of various kinds teaches the young and the old alike, to appreciate or develop an aversion for different types of values. The appreciation or aversion of a particular type of value is of course determined by the 'sub-culture' of the neighbourhood, in which the person lives. For example, in a slum where the social fabric is fairly loose, lax social controls and unstable social interactions, disorderly ways of doing things, irregular attendance at school or working place and unclean surroundings, may well enjoy social tolerance. But in a neighbourhood where people who belong to a particular 'class' or status, which values the concept of a well-ordered social existance, the values tolerated in a slum environment may be abhorred. In a neighbourhood where there is a strong social disapproval for anti-social conduct, people live and function with a sense of responsibility, which generally acts as a check against indulging in those activities which are detrimental to social well-being.

In a multi-religious society like ours, the study of religion as a major base for value development assumes special significance. Children are inculcated into certain values through religion even at a very young age. Religion is increasingly becoming a source of 'identifying' oneself as well as others. It is a powerful factor in inculcating as well as strengthening values. If not tackled properly, religious agencies can do more harm than good. Religious affiliations being sensitive issues could create more rifts than social cohesion, if the broad universal aspects and the great common ideals of all religions are taught most intensively and pervasively, right from the beginning. In many countries including India today, religious fundamentalism and narrow loyalties have greatly disturbed the traditional social adjustment and understanding. Human beings are set against other human beings simply because they profess allegiance to different religions. Negative values like hatred, intolerance and violence are being fostered in the name of religion. Religion, which should act as a unifying factor, under some circumstances has emerged as the greatest divider. As a powerful and reinforcing influence, religion could help in spreading the right kind of values that could generate immense social good. Values like tolerance, love of truth, spirit of sacrifice, fellow-feeling etc. could be inculcated through religious precepts in a very effective manner.

Education is one of the basic institutions through which every society sustains itself as well as transmits its values to posterity. Durkheim (1956) sees education as the process of methodical socialisation of the young. Education, in this context has two important functions to perform, the first of which relates to maintaining 'social stability' and the other tends to ushering in 'social change'. While preparing the young and old alike for accepting new ideas and new values, education also transmits from one generation to the other such values which function as the very basis of society's survival. Values like honesty, integrity, discipline, desire for knowledge, social justice are universal in their nature and must be inculcated in every type of social system. At the same time, society is not static and must continually absorb within itself new ideas and changes. Irrelevant, ill-conceived and immobile values must be rejected and replaced without any hesitation, and education plays a very constructive role in the spread of the right kind of values. Our reference to an educational institution would encompas both the formal and informal agencies of education. Formal education which is represented by schools, colleges and other institutions of learning covering a large section of the common people, symbolise the hopes and aspirations of many in the modern world. It serves as the most important avenue for social mobility. Besides imparting knowledge, the formal educational institutions should also inculcate qualities such as leadership, peaceful co-exixtence, mutual tolegance and respect for others rights. In schools particularly, the young are exposed to two dominant and long-lasting influences. One is the association with the fellow students and the other, contact with the teachers. While fellow students could provide role-models, ideas as well as guidence, teachers, on the other hand provide the most strong and stable source of support and encouragement to their students. The teachers try to inculcate in their students a strong commitment to those values which are good for the students as well as the society in general.

In this way the school is a very important source of value development. The school has to wean the young away from those values which are detrimental to social and individual well-being. The youth today are exposed to a set of conflicting values and are not certain about the type of values they have to choose from within the society itself forces like corruption, religious fundamentalism, casteism tendencies are misguiding our youth. The school has to combat these forces and provide to the young alternate role models which can lead them to the right direction. If schools fail in this task of inculcating the right kind of values, it might spell disaster for the posterity.

If the school is a powerful base of formal education, the mass media are the most influential among the informal agencies of education. The mass media do not directly involve interpersonal interaction. They with their content alone teach many of the ways which are characteristics of a given society. The communication imparted through the mass media teach the individuals the norms, the social position and the institutional functions. The recurrent themes and stories continue to present values and ideals associated with particular status and sex and as such play a powerful role in value transmission.

Values are realted to personal, social, moral, aesthetic and spiritual behaviours. They are quite internalized structures. Morality forms the base of the value system one cherishes. It has a social reference and the conscience primarily emerges from morality. Values are basically affective in the sense that a strong feeling is central to a value. But it has also a cognitive and conative dimensions. It tends to imply that while a strong feeling is key to any value, its base lies in one's system of knowledge and beliefs, and tends to induce certain form of behaviours.

None is born with values or morality. They are acquired, learnt and developed. Values develop through one's experience in life, through the different socio-cultural interactions. Such experiences make for certain meanings, expectancies and interpretations with value content.

Different psychologists have advanced descriptive theories of moral development. They present stage-wise descriptions of qualitative changes. Given below is a brief outline of the features of each.

JEAN PIAGET AND MORAL DEVELOPMENT

Piaget (1960) tried to study the developmental aspects of children's moral beliefs and knowledge. His theory moral development outlines that individuals attain development of moral reasoning through heteronomous morality in early and middle childhood (3-8 years) and autonomus morality beyond this stage., The stage or heteronomous morality is characterised by moral realism. egocentricism and absolutism. Moral realism refers to that acts are being judged by their consequences and not by the intention that give rise to them. Egocentricism tends to mean the inability of the child to distinguish his own views from that of others which in turn leads to an inability to consider or accept others' viewpoints It simply means that the child's own interests are being generalised and sought. To Piaget (1960) absolutism means that children view moral rules as fixed and believe that the rules can never be changed.

With the development of intellectual capacities the children gradually assume independence in moral judgements and the unquestioned respect for adults is changed into mutual considerations and respect, equality and social cooperation. Thus the child attains the level of autonomy in moral development. An act is judged by the intent rather than by its consequences. They consider neither the rules as absolute nor adults views as always right. The rules are treated as flexible. The children are quite aware of the possible diversity of views existing among people about right and wrong. Thus, children at the stage of 'autonomous morality' judge an act as bad by intentions and rationality.

L.KOHLBERG AND MORAL DEVELOPMENT

Kohlbern (1963, 1964, 1969) elaborated Piaget's theory to demonstrate moral development as a continuous process. His theory of moral development is based on the ideas originally formulated by Piaget Kohlberg (1963) originally identified six stages in the moral development and grouped them into three levels. His revised theory has three levels and five stages—the pre-conventional (stages 1 and 2),—conventional (stages 3 and 4) and post—conventional (stage-5).

PRE CONVENTIONAL LEVEL

Stage-1 : Heteronomous Morality

In this stage morality is oriented to obedience and punishment. Any behaviour which is immoral is punished. In contrast a behaviour moral because it does not get punished. The morality of the child is determined by the consequences of an action. It implies that the child obeys rules to avoid punishment. The child's moral behaviour is under external control.

Stage-2 : Individualism and Exchange

This is the stage when moral actions are directed to further child's own interest and allow others to do the same. For a child, which is right or good is what satisfies him/her. To gain something from others, children understand that they must recognise and respond to others' needs. The morality is based upon the outlook: you scratch my back and I will scratch yours.

CONVENTIONAL LEVEL

Stage-3 : Mutual Expectations and Interpersonal Conformity

This is the stage when conventional morality begins. At this stage children value relationships based on mutual trust and loyalty. Behaviour to be good must please others. Children are more oriented to win the approval of others and to avoid their disapproval. They try to live up to the expectations of people close to them and try to fulfil the different roles. More importance is given to mutual agreements and individual interest takes a back seat. The children develop the tendency to see things from others' perspective and show genuine care for others.

Stage-4 : Social System

One's moving into this stage possesses conventional morality at a higher level. Morality is based on abstract understanding of society as a whole. It emphasises meeting social and religious responsibilities, upholding the law and contributing to the society. Individuals at this stage accept social conventions and rules, and preserve social structure. Morality puts emphasis on doing one's duty, showing respect for authority and maintaining the existing social order.

POST-CONVENTIONAL LEVEL

Stage-5 : Social Contract

This is the stage when moral behaviour becomes increasingly internal. Individuals at this stage believe that the purpose of the law is to preserve human rights. Moral behaviour relies on an agreement among individuals to conform to laws that are necessary for the human welfare. The question on the need and process of determining laws by the society. They know well that the laws are outcome of social contract and should be followed. But law and social commitments are not accepted blindly rather laws are examined on the basis of the greatest good for the greatest number. On this ground individuals see that the laws should be obeyed. But a given law may be rejected if it violates the intrinsic worth and dignity of individuals. They are highly oriented to rational judgements, human rights, social commitments and justice etc.

Kohlberg (1969) sees moral development as a progression from stage 1 to 5 where each succeeding stage needs higher perspective than the preceding stage.

R.F. PECK AND R.J. HAVINGHURST AND MORAL DEVELOPMENT

From their study, Peck and Havinghurst (1960) found fived stages of character development. They are :

(i) a moral,
(ii) expedient,
(iii) conforming,
(iv) irrational-conscientious
(v) rational altruistic types.

The moral type has an infantile inability to control himself in social situations The expendient type conforms in order to avoid adult punishment or disapproval.

The conforming type goes along passively with the social and moral value. Such a person is said to have a crude conscience with not generalized sense of morality over varied situatons. The irrational-conscientious type lives by absolute rules but has been forced to internalize them more completely and rigidly than the conformer. The rational altruistic is described by Peck and Havinghurst (1960) as the highest level of moral maturity. The individual makes a rational assessment of experience, and has formed his principles. He reacts with emotion appropriate to the occasion as against passive conformity.

LOEVINGER AND MORAL DEVELOPMENT

Loevinger (1966) has evolved a model of ego development which is related to all the concepts discussed above and a number of concepts proposed by others. Ego development in this model is a central construct related to moralization (Kohlberg, 1964), character development (Peck and havinghurst, 1960). Interpersonel integration (Sullivan, Grant and Grant, 1957), conceptual systems (Harvey, Hunt and Shroeder, 1961), Intraception (Murray, 1938) and so on.

Loevinger's stages of ego development includes :

1. **Pre-social Symbolic** : The problem for the child is to distinguish self from non-self.
2. **Impulse-ridden** : The child confirms his separate existence from the mother by the exercise of his own will.
3. **Opportunistic** : At this stage rules are obeyed in terms of immediate advantage. Thus the morality is purely an expedient one. There is a marked shift from independence as in stage-2.
4. **Coformist** : This stage is characterised by partial internalization of rules. Internal-personal relations are seen mainly in terms of actions rather than of feelings and motives.
5. **Conscientious** : At this stage morality has been internalized. Inner and more imperatives supersede group sanctioned rules Inter-personal relations are seen in terms of beliefs and traits rather than actions.
6. **Autonomous** : The characterstic moral issue at this stage is coping with inner conflict, conflicting duties, conflicting needs, conflict between needs and duties, and so on.
7. **Integrated** : The person proceeds beyond coping with conflict to reconciliation of conflicting demands and where necessary, renunciation of the unattainable. According to this hierarchical view the individual tends to start off poorly controlled, self-centred, and develops through successive stages to the point where he proceeds beyond coping with conflict to reconciliation of conflicting demands and cherishing of individual differences; and beyond role differentiation to the achievement of a sense of integrated indentity.

Loevinger's (1966) invariant sequence paradigm is most model of similar to Piaget's (1960) model of congnitive development and Kohlberg's (1963) scheme of moral development.

A.H. MASLOW AND MORAL DEVELOPMENT

Maslow (1956) ascribes the development of character traits, cognitive, conative-affective, and interpersonal development to the gratification of basic needs. He proposes a need hierarchy in which emergence of higher level needs is subject to the gratification of lower level needs. To him needs can be ordered as follows : (i) Physiological, (ii) Safety, (iii) Love, (iv) Esteem, and (v) Self -actualization.

An individual's feelings values, attitudes, character traits, aspiration level, intuitive powers, and social abilities develop in certain ways on the basis of the pattern of need gratification or need frustration.

N.J BULL AND MORAL DEVELOPMENT

Bull (1966) proposed four stages of moral development : anomy, heteronomy, socionomy and autonomy. He conceives moral development as progression from one stage to another with certain degree of overlapping between stages. His stages of moral development are tied to chronological age development.

'Anomy' is period of pre-moral stage. This is the beginning stage in life and the infant has no sense of morality or immorality. An infant is a moral at this stage.

'Heteronomy', the next stage, is marked by child's obedience to external control. The behaviour of the child is controlled and disciplined by adults using reward and punishments mechanisms. Thus, morality at this stage is determined by external control with the intention to develop self-discipline.

'Socionomy' being the third stage is characterised by external-internal control. At this stage the child becomes conscious of himself and tries to establish healthy relationship with peers and others in the society. Need for affiliation to the group is increasingly high and peer group influences assume greater dominance. Family, school, peer group, association and club are important for the socialisation of the actions of the child using reward and punishment; Praise and reproof, and approval and disapproval mechanisms. Through this process of socialisation the child accepts and follows the rules, regulations and conventions governing the society. In this way, morality is shaped by social forces.

'Autonomy' is the stage of internal moral development. The individuals at this stage develops conscience and tries to follow the moral codes. Individuals become self-disciplined and actions are regulated by conscience. With the progress of consience, individuals become capable of taking moral decisions independently and gradually replace external and control by the corresponding internal control.

At these theories of moral development which we have discussed are consistent and complementary to each other. For example, when Piaget (1960) and Kohlberg (1969) focus on the basis and nature of moral judgement at successive stages, Bull (1966) stressed the sources of influence or control.

3

REVIEW OF THE LITERATURE

It is worthwhile for a researcher to make a comprehensive survey of what has already been done on the problem and its related aspects. The purpose of the review of literature is to build up in the context and background of the research as well as to provide a basis for formulation of the hypotheses. Since a good research is based upon everything that is known in the area of research, the review of research provides to this effect. For progress to occur, it is essential that new work be based and built on what has already been accomplished. In this context, Mouly (1964) states, "Survey of related literature avoids the risk of duplication, provides theories, ideas, explanations or hypotheses valuable in formulating the problem and contributes to the general scholarship of the investigator".

Values as empirical elements in human behaviour certainly arise out of human experience and hence may be affected by any condition, the condition may be social, political, religious, economic, psychological or educational that affect experience. Values may, therefore, be analysed as dependent variables, subject to changes that are consequent to changes in population, technology, economic production, political organisation and so on. Once established however, values operate as independent variables, serving as basis for further researches and innovations. Hence both types of studies are available in which values are treated dependent as well as independent variables. In the present research, the investigator has scanned most of the relevant and reported studies done in India and abroad in the field of values. The present chapter provides a thumb nail account of such studies, their ambit and outcomes.

STUDIES CONDUCTED ABROAD

The investigator has reviewed a large number of studies conducted in the area of values. However, a review of the available research related to the variable and various comparison groups included in the present study is given below.

Values and Achievement

Value is important in the learning process because it influences selection of the stimuli to which the learner responds, the rapidity of learning, retention of the learned response, and application of the learned materials. Theoretically, one's values must constitute an important source of behavioural motivation. School learning is also an aspect of behaviour. In few researches abroad attempts have been made to analyse the relationship between values and academic performance of the students.

Dewinter (1961) in order to measure the similarity in values between a group of college students and their instructors and to relate this similarity to their academic achievement in his class took 34 freshers (men) enrolled in a required course in general psychology taught by the same male instructor. A modified form of the semantic Differential as described by Osgood and his co-workers was the instrument used to measure values. The findings of the study were (i) grade achievement was significantly related to the ACE—linguistic and total score and to the degree of similarity in value between student and professor, (ii) in addition, grades were also significantly correlated with the student's ability to correctly predict his instructor's values, (iii) Father's education and the quantitative score of the ACE were correlated with grades, while mother's education showed a small but not significant correlation with the criterion, (iv) the two best predictors of class achievement were the student professor discrepancy score and the ACE—Linguistic score and (v) the value discrepancy and academic aptitude measures appear to be distinct variables, although each correlates with grade.

Thomson (1961) reported that the grades earned by the students appeared to be related to personal values and the students making the highest grades to be those with emergent kinds of values.

Dewinter (1962) studied student values and grades in general psychology by taking 42 non-freshmen college students (24 men and 18 women) enrolled in a course in general psychology taught by the same instructor as in the previous study. The result revealed that three of the four predictions were confirmed. Grade achievement was related to degree of similarity between the values of the student and his instructor to the investigator of the students' democratic unprejudiced and broadminded values, and to his intelligence. The pattern of intercorrelations among these three predictors variables indicated a positive relationship between intelligence and democratic values on the E-F scale, the E-F scale and student—professor discrepancy are moderately correlated, indicating that to some extent having values similar to the instructors means having democratic and non-ethnocentric values. The 90 score was not highly correlated with student-professor discrepancy and these appear to the disparate factors, although each correlates with grades and to some extent with E-F score. In any case the three variables (IQ. EF & student—professor discrepancy) all correlates with achievement although the correlations with each other was complex, the fourth prediction that grades would be correlated with the student's ability to predict the professor's value rankings was not confirmed.

Cattell, Sealey and Sweney (1966) made a study on the basis of which they generalised that value patterns operated strongly in the interaction of pupils and teachers and hence it was quite reasonable to think that pupil's patterns of values were related to the level of pupil's school learning.

Cole and Miller (1967) conducted a study on male and female college students and concluded that academic achievement is significantly related to the values of students.

Walker (1970) worked on values and found that the students of high scholastic achievement expressed higher traditional values than those of low scholastic achievement.

Hapner (1970) made an attempt to examine if success and failure of divergent ethnic groups can be related to discrepancies in values between them and the schools in which they are expected to function. The investigation uncovered significant differences in values between Mexican-American and Anglo-American boys which influence their educational behaviour and achievements.

Bellucci (1970) reported that none of the values was significantly related to scores obtained by the trainees in nursing training programmes. Leadership was the only value giving significant correlation with completion of the practical nursing programme.

The study of Mulder (1974) showed that value systems of students differed according to grade level of students. Value systems of students and teachers differed at all four grade levels. Greater differences existed between value systems of teachers and low achieveing students. Value systems of students differed according to the achievement level of students. Few differences exsited between value of parents according to age level of parents. Few differences existed in values of teachers according to age level of teachers. Value systems of students differed from value system of parents. Few differences existed between the value of teachers and students when compared to SES of the parents of the students. Few differences existed in values of students according to the SES of their parents. Value systems of students differed according to the religious orientation of teachers. Few differences existed in the values of parents according to the religious orientation of parents.

Soble (1978) conducted a study on students value change and congruency with faculty values in professional education. The findings demostrated that there was no significant academic differences between students who were congruent and non-congruent with faculty.

Arccnaaw (1990) compared college students exhibiting discrepancies between predicted high ability and low level of achievement. In comparing results, the three achievements groups differed consistently on all measures, with the majority of differences involving socialization or conformity—A conflict exists for the low and high achievers in meeting the societal expectations for achievement with their own individual interests and values. This suggests that extremes of achievement among college students, in either direction, should generate concern as high achievers may be meeting expectations at the expense of other facets of their lives. A gender difference was noted with the low-achieveing group predominantly male and the high achieving group predominantly female. However, for both groups gender differences could be accounted for by an over representation by one gender within the sample group.

Comparative Studies

A good number of scholars such as Glickman and Whol (1965), Garden (1966), Sundberg *et al.*(1970) Beg (1966), Convas (1971), Garsee and Glixman (1971), Kakkar and Kibly (1971), and Pourier (1977) have tried to study the cross cultural effect on the values of students. These studies reported some significant differences in the values of students belonging to different cultures. On the other hand Begum and Hafees (1964) found no relationship of values with caste and religion. Cameron and Robertson (1970) reported that similarities appeared much mark than dissimilarities, in the values between Scot and US, Children. Sharman (1971) reported that there were no difference between values of negro and white students. Huntley (1958) reported that there was a significant gain on the aesthetic values and corresponding decrease on the religious vlaues during the four years of college for all the curricular groups.

Entwistle (1972) found that students of different type of institutions (College of Education, Polytechnics, Language, Pure Science, Applied Sciences, Mathematics) differed in their values.

Davidson (1970) and Gibson (1978) compared the value traits of athlets and non-athletes. The findings of these studies revealed that significant differences were found to exist between athletes and non-athletes on the value classification.

Herrick (1978) found that there were significant differences values of students entering in the college of business and the students about to complete college degree.

Many researchers have studied sex differences in vlaues. The study of Wartz, Nolman and Tillman (1962) showed a correlation of 97 when compared the relative ranking of the ten values items of the fourth grade girls' with fourth grade boys'ranking. The boys and girls differed only sligntly. The girls ranked fairly life as the number one vlaue with friendship number two. The boys reversed these two values with friendship having the highest ranking. The power and control values was ranked ninth. But the girls ranked recognition tenth and power and control ninth. The remaining six items were given the same relative position of importance by both groups.

The seventh grade girls correlated 75 with the seventh grade boys on their ranking of the ten value items. Both groups ranked friendship and family life one and two respectively. Both groups agreed on excitement and recreation (6th), privacy (7th), recognition (9th) and power and control (10th). The boys ranked comfort and relaxation number three with personal improvement being, fifth. The girls reversed these two categories. Beauty ranked fourth and physical freedom (8th) by the girls, but these were 8th and 4th respectively in case of boys. A correlation of 94 was obtained when comparing the composite fourth and seventh grades.

The fourth and seventh grades ranked friendship as the most important value, followed by family life and personal improvement. Both groups ranked beauty 5th, recognition 9th and power and control 10th. Excitement and recreation was 4th rank to the fourth graders with comfort and relaxation 4th with excitement and recreation 6th. Further the fourth grade ranked privacy 7th and physical freedom 8th whereas the seventh graders reversed the relative position of these two values.

A study conducted by Nolman, Bran and Tillman (1963) showed that the mean, SD and range of the California F—scale scores for each of the twelve classes used in the study varies form 118.31 to 146.07, 14.86 to 23.16 and 68 to 190 respectively. Negative correlation were found for the theoretical, aesthetic, political and religious sub-scales (for males). All were significant at the .01 level of confidence.

The social sub-scale (male) was also negatively correlated with significance at the .05 level. The only female sub-scale which correlated significantly with F-scale was the aesthetic which was negatively correlated at the .01 level. Significant differences at the .01 level were found for the aesthetic social, political, religious correlations. When the combined male and female scores on the Allport—Vernon were correlated with the F-scale score, three sub-scales, *i.e.*, theoretical the aesthetic and the political were found to be significat at the .01 level (but negatively). The religious correlation was also negative at the 0.5 level.

The Allport-vernon scores was significant at .01 level for the theoretical, economic, social, political and religious sub-scales. The aesthetic sub-scale was significant at the the .01 level.

Of special interest is the fact that the lowest mean F-scale was found for the college preparatory class and the highest mean F-scale for the remedial english class. The difference between these means was significant at the 0.1 level.

In 1971, Loustein wanted to investigate the relationship between self-esteem and personal values in high school students. The study was an 'expost facto' study. For this purpose a total sample of 1720 students from two high schools Illionis were drawn. Pearson product moment correlation coefficients were calculated for the population as a whole, for each sex and for each grade level in order to study the relationship of self-esteem to each of the six personal values and to each of the six interpersonal values. For seniors, self-esteem, correlated to the degree of 0.21 with the personal value of achievement. All other correlation's coefficients for the personal values and interpersonal vlaues not observed to be significantly different from zero.

Another study was conducted by the same author, Loustein (1972) to study any change in personal and interpersonal. Values of high school adolescents by grade, sex and occupational group. He found a significant main effort for occupation and the null hypothesis was rejected for the occupational groups. However the null hypothesis was retained for the effect of sex and grade.

Significant main effects occurred for both sex and occupational group resulting interaction of the null hypothesis for these two variables and the retention of the null hypothesis for the effect of grades. The mean for males 15-52 was significantly higher than the mean of females 14.15.

Significat results were obtained for the sex and grade dimensions. But the null hypothesis was retained for the occupational groups.

With the purpose of determining whether significant differences exist in the measured values of elementary school children in grades four, five and six in relation to the variables of sex grade parochial school and public school students and socio-economic level as measured by the social values Inventory (SVI), Silvino (1973) took a total of 555 children from two public schools and two parochial schools. The findings of the study revealed that male and female students do differ in what values they consider important as measured by the SVI. The value categories that seem to produce the differences were pleasure, materialism, occupation, achievement and environmental. Students in grade four, five and six differ in what value they consider important as measured by the SVI. The value categorises that seem to produce the differences were religion, health, independence, and achievement. Parochial school and public school students differ in what vlaues they consider important as measured by the SVI. The value categories of equality seems to produce the difference.

STUDIES CONDUCTED IN INDIA

Many scholars in India have studied values in relation to some other variables. A few Indian studies have been presented below with a view to have proper knowledge in the concerned field.

Values and Achievement

In India situation the research studies on the values in relation to achievement are death. However the available Indian studies are presented below.

A study was undertaken by Makhija (1973) to inquire into the interaction among values, interests and intelligence and its impact on scholastic achievement. For the purpose a stratified random sample of 310 first year male students studying in the faculties of arts, science, commerce and agriculture was drawn. The major findings of the study were : (i) Intelligence had a significantly positive influence on scholastic achievement. (ii) Students who were not oriented to political value, exploited their mental ability to much less extent than those who were highly oriented to it. (iii) Students who valued beauty from symmetry and grade in their life developed vocational interests in literary pursuit and avoided, as far as possible, sports and outdoor activities. (iv) Students who were oriented to practical and utilitarian view of life tended to exert their intellectual capacities more in the mechanical fields of vocations. (v) Students who valued power, competition, renown, etc., in their life utilised their mental abilities to excel in crafts and scientific studies. (vi) Students whose ideas of life was to probe in to the mysteries of God, exploited their intelligence in the fields of science and medicine. (vii) Adolescent boys motivated by affection, friendship and love of people used their intelligence in household activities. (viii) Those who cherished search of truth as the dominant ideal of life would not divert their capacities to mechanical occupations. (ix) None of the six values had any significant influence on scholastic achievement. (x) The motive to gain power as a means to dominant, control and influence others accelerated scholastic achievement. (xi) Intelligent students interested in science and medicine found religious value helpful in their performance but obstructive if they were interested in recreational activities. (xii) Students highly interested in sports seldom proved high achievers in schools interest in the medical field had no relevance to scholastic achievement; their interest was mostly induced extraneously by family and society. There was affinity between religious value and technical interest and they jointly influenced the calibre of the student in respect of his scholastic achievement.

Rajput (1985) attempted to ascertain whether faculty-wise different predictor variables, *i.e.* Values, dependency, academic adjustment and socio-economic status of the parents, made a differential impact. The findings of the study were :

(i) **Father's Occupation** ; Fathers education and academic achievement in science, social reconstruction, and mathematics, arithmetic, appeared to contribute meaningfully to faculty differences.

(ii) From among six values considered, only theoretical value appeared to be responsible for faculty differences.

(iii) Social value, mothers education and achievement in Gujarati were responsible for sex differences.

(iv) The achievement in Gujarati and mathematics/arithmetic appeared to be predictive of sex differences.

(v) Except in the case of values sexwise differences were more or less absent in the commerce and science faculties.

(vi) With respect to the faculty of arts, no meaningful pattern appeared for values, SES of the parents and academic achievement.

(vii) SES for both boys and girls appeared to be unidimensional in the science faculty.

(viii) SES appeared to be bi-dimensional with respect to both boys and girls in the commerce faculty. Income and father's occupation formed one component. Father's and mother's education formed the other component.

(ix) Dependence proneness was not at all meaningfully related to academic achievement.

(x) Academic adjustment was not meaningfully related to academic achievement.

Rath (1994) undertook a study on the attitude and values in relation to achievement of IX graders. The value test of Agarwal, translated into oriya by Panda (1990) was used to measure the values of the students. The major findings of the study were :

(i) There were significant differences of values between the high achievers and low achievers.

(ii) Values possessed in the dimension of personal, educational, materialistic of high achievers were more than the low achievers.

(iii) Values possessed by low achievers in the areas of religious, socialistic and humanistic were more than the high achievers.

(iv) There was significant relationship between various dimensions of values and achievement excepting religious value.

In order to study the academic achievement and value pattern of the best athletes of Vidya Bharati Verma and Srivastava (1997) took up a study. They found that female athletes taken together at national level were significantly higher in their academic achievement in comparison to the male athletes. Gender difference was also found to be significant in the case of Rajasthan athletes where female Rajasthani athletes had shown significantly higher academic achievement in comparison to their male counterparts from the same state. In case of Haryana state the male athletes were significantly superior in comparison to their female counterpart in academic achievement. It was found that at national as well as state levels patriotism (Des Bhakti), social and knowledge values occupied the top three ranks respectively in schools run by Vidya Bharati. The bottom three ranks were occupied by economic, aesthetic and religious values respectively. Health and power values were in the middle on knowledge and social values at national level girls were significantly higher than boys. On economic value boys belonging to Bihar, Madhya Pradesh and Rajasthan were significantly higher than their female counterparts from the same state. On health value boys of Rajasthan were found to be significantly higher than the girls. But on social values girls from Bihar and Rajasthan were significantly higher than their male counterparts. In the same vain girls of Rajasthan were significantly superior than their male counterparts in patriotic value.

Comparative Studies

There are several studies in India in which attempts have been made to compare value patterns terms of sex, grade, culture, residential back ground, profession and socio-economic status. Such studies are quite germane to understand the nature of value and have been presented in the following pages.

In order to study the social background of college students, their attitudes, values and preferences, Saxena (1972) took 500 students of Jhansi. The study revealed :

(i) The majority of the students had highest reference for creative literature and fairly high preference for scientific literature.

(ii) In films educational films, musical and religious films were liked the most, light music and film music were most popular among the college students.

(iii) The majority of the boys aspired for technical jobs as engineers and doctors while girls preferred medicine and teaching as a profession.

(iv) Students were open to intercaste and intereligious marriage.

(v) On tradition and modernity index, the students stood midway, and on sacred and secular measure they were overwhelmingly, secular. They opted for social participation and had kin-oriented outlook.

(vi) The girls led a more protected life restricted movements; the girls and the boys differed in responses to items on the place visited, living and eating arrangements, martial status, social and economic background and courses offered.

(vii) While the male students preferred scientific literature, sports and news over the radio, girls preferred novels and radio dramas.

(viii) The conception of feminine roles also contributed to the girls choice of medicine and teaching as professions.

(ix) The faculty wise (arts/science) differences were found limited to the scientific attitude, movie and music preferences, man-nature and man-man-relationship, but the faculty had a profound effect on preference for reading and the choice of occupation.

(x) The educational levels also differentiated the students; intermediate students demonstrated dreaminess, greater idealism, and a more normative influence on their attitude with less sense of realism and greater optimism, where as the students in the degree level hand greater realism maturity of thought, and a sense of frustration.

(xi) Longer exposure to education seemed to contribute to better and realistic outlook to situations and life.

Katiyar (1976) studied the values of the Intermediate class students in relation to vocational preferences. The study was conducted on 2158 urban male students of sevel cities of U.P. The findings of the study were :

(i) The students were high in domestic, social and knowledge value, Medium in health, religious, family prestige and aesthetic values and low in power, hedonistic and economic values.

(ii) The value system of the students of the five courses were very much similar. Inter-group differences shaved that mathematics and biology students were higher in social, democratic, knowledge and aesthetic values than arts, commerce and agriculture students. They were also higher than agriculture students in economic value-Mathematics students were higher than commerce students in hedonists value.

(iii) Hindu students were higher than Muslim students in social value.

(iv) Students of high Hindu caste groups except low Hindu caste group, they were higher than the low castes in social, aesthetic and knowledge values; than lower middle caste in aesthetic and poor values, than the middle caste in social, aesthetic, economic, knowledge and poor values and than upper middle caste in poor family prestige health values.

(v) The students of very high income group were higher than very low, lower middle and middle income groups in aesthetic, economic and knowledge values and they were also higher than upper middle group in economic value.

(vi) The students of very high fathers education group were higher than that of very low and low groups in social democratic, aesthetic and knowledge values than below average, average and above average groups in aesthetic value, than below average group in knowledge value and than high group in health value.

(vii) The students of very high fathers profession group were higher than below average group in social value, than all except very low group in hedonistic value, than very low, low below average and average groups in aesthetic value and than low, below average and above average groups in knowledge value.

(viii) With respect the vocational preferences, it was found that executive physical sciences and linguistic were highly preferred biological sicences, humanitarian, persuasive and business were moderately preferred and computational, artistic and musical were less preferred.

(ix) The students' high vocational preferences were directly related with their courses.

(x) Hindu students were higher than Muslim students in musical, Muslim students were higher than Hindu students in persuasive and Christian students were higher than Hindu and Muslim students in musical field.

(xi) Executive and physical sciences fields were highly preferred by all the students.

(xii) The relationship was found positive and significant of religious value with computational, persuasive, humanitarian, and musical fields of social value with physical sciences biological sciences, persuasive, humanitarian. Musical fields of democratic value with physical sciences, biological sciences and humanitarian fields, of aesthetic value with physical sciences, artistic and musical fields, of economic value with computational and business fields, of knowledge value with physical sciences, biological sciences and linguistic fields of power value with computational, business and executive fields, of hedonistic value with artistic and musical fields of family prestige value with computational, executive and persuasive fields and of health value with biological sciences, linguistic and humanitarian fields.

(xiii) The relationship was found negative and significant of religious value with physical sciences and biological sciences of social value with computational and artistic fields of democratic value with business and artistic fields, of aesthetic value with biological sicences, computational, persuasive and humantarian fields of economic value with physical sciences, biological sciences lingustic and humanitarian fields of knowledge value with computational business and persuasive fields of hedonistic value with computational and humanitarian fields of power value with biological sciences and linguistic fields of family prestige value with physical sciences, artistic and musical fields and health value with computational and business fields.

Sharma (1977) reported that the mean differences between the male and female high school students was significant only in the case of the theoretical value. No significant differences were found in the case of other values namely, political, social, religious, economic and aesthetic. There was no significant difference between the mean scores of male and the female high school teachers on social, religious, economic, aesthetic, theoretical values whereas in the case of social, aesthetic and political values. However, the mean scores of the male teachers were higher than those of their female counterparts on religious, economic and theoretical value whereas in the case of social, aesthetic and political value their mean scores were lower than those of the female teachers. The mean scores of the male teachers were higher on social and economic values than those of their students but were lower than those of their students on the religious value. The mean difference between the male teachers and their female students was significant on the political value.

On the remaining values no significant difference was found. There was a significant mean difference between the high school female teachers and their male students on the aesthetic value. On the remaining values no significant differences were found. The male university students scored higher on theoretical and political values than their female counterparts. The mean difference between the male teachers and their male students of the university was significant on religious and political values. No significant differences were found on social, economic, aesthetic and theoretical values. The mean difference between the female teachers and their female students of the university was significant on social and theoretical values. However, there was no significant difference in the case of religious, economic, aesthetic and political values. The mean difference between the male teachers and the female students of the university was found to be significant for the theoretical value. On economic and aesthetic values the female teachers mean score was significantly higher than that of their male students whereas on the political value the mean score of the male students was significantly higher than that of their female teachers.

Reddy (1980) attempted to know the differences in the perceptions of values and attitudes of the youth of different backgrounds (rural and urban). The study reported the following findings;

(i) The rate of acquisition of modern attitudes with the increase in age was higher in the urban students than in the rural ones. The rural subjects were more traditionalistic than the urban subjects, especially in the areas of home and hetero-sexual relations.

(ii) The rural students were more politically oriented than the urban group. The migrant-urban students were least satisfied with the present educational system closely followed by the urban students.

(iii) The adolescents living in joint families revealed more traditional attitude than those coming from nuclear families.

(iv) The students coming from homes with higher socio-economic status expressed more modern attitudes than those coming from lower-status homes.

(v) The students with the deprived educational background were more favourable inclined to political participation than those with higher educational backgrounds.

(vi) The boys were found to be more non-conforming than the girls. The urban students were found to be more conforming than the rural and the migrant-urban students.

(vii) The rural students were more close-minded than the urban or migrant-urban students.

(viii) The boys were found showing preference to political, theoretical and economic values while the girls to aesthetic, religious and social values.

(ix) Economic status and political and theoretical values elicited greater favourable response from subjects with comparatively low socio-economic status whereas aesthetic and religious values were more important to the higher socio-economic group.

(x) The rural students showed greater perference for theoretical, economic, political and social values whereas their urban counterparts were more inclined to aesthetic and religious values.

Sahgal (1980) found that the co-educationals showed significant change in personality factors at the end of the year of their collegiate life. They became more reserved, detached, cool and cautious in their emotional expression. The non-coeducational also experienced a significant change. They became less assertive and showed proneness to giving way to others, were less sober and showed significant tendency towards conscientiousness, showed satisfactory faith in their own decisions as well as the decisions of other and a tendency towards satisfactory control over their emotions. With respect to the differences in the change in personality of the coeducational and of the non-coeducational differed significantly. The coeducationals became significantly more reserved, cool and cautions in their emotional expression than the non-coeducational. Improvement in the overall self-concept and its intellectual, social and aesthetic dimensions was observed among one coeducational. They perceived themselves significantly more wise, systematic, intelligent, critical, curious, argumentative, efficient, precise, competent having clear thinking and inventive spirits, likeable polite, open-minded, co-operative and friendly, social humorous, graceful, artistic, attractive and sophisticated. On the other hand the non-coeducational showed significant improvement in their overall self concept. The co-educational described themselves as more attractive and graceful than the non-coeducational. The economic and health value of the coeducational showed a significant change. At the end of the third year, the economic values of these students significantly deteriorated. The non-coeducationals showed gradual but significant improvement in their aesthetic and health values. The non-coeducational developed significantly more liking for decoration of the home and surroundings, neatness and system in the arrangement of things than the coeducationals. In respect to the health values, the coeducational showed less importance to them at the end of the third year. The deterioration in the knowledge value of the coeducational was significantly more than that of the non-coeducationals.

Patel (1981) found that students became more sociable with their increase in age. The older students were more involved in economic values than the younger ones. The girl students scored higher than the boy students on rational values. In religious values the higher income girl students scored higher than the higher income boy students. In scientific values lower income urban students scored higher than the higher income urban students. Student of both the sexes and both the standards scored high for moral value. However, the lower income rural students scored higher than the lower income urban students. The majority of the students liked to be active in aesthetic or art-oriented activities. Here, the girl students scored higher than the boy students. The girl scored higher than the boys on religious, moral and scientific values. On economic, moral, political and aesthetic values, the students of std. XI scored higher than the students of standard X.9. On all other values, except the rational and the political, the urban students scored higher than the rural students. On social, rational and moral values, students with lower income scored higher than students with higher income.

Kalia (1982) conducted a study on values and ideals of early adolescents living in different types of home environment and found that the both parent, male adolescents scored significantly higher on theoretical and political values than those from orphan homes, who excelled in aesthetic and religious values. The former were higher in physical, educational, political and economic ideals and the latter scored higher on family and sports ideals. The both-parent males and one-parents males were similar in their theoretical, economic, aesthetic, political and religious value. Preferences, whereas Social values were found higher in the case of the both-parent, subjects. The both-parent early adolescent males scored higher on physical educational political and economic ideals, whereas, orphans scored higher on family and sports ideals. The one-parent male subjects scored significantly higher on theoretical and political values and excelled in physical, political, and economic ideas, whereas those from orphanages gave high rating to social and religious values and sports ideals. No significant difference was found between the both-parent and the one-parent females in values except in political values in which the former scored significantly higher. In the case of ideas the former group was found higher on physical, educational and political ideas and the latter group on family and sports ideals. The both-parents female respondents were found significantly higher on theoretical and religoius values than those from orphanages who scored higher on aesthetic and social values of female respondents from orphan homes and from one-parent homes except on theoretical value, in which the former group lagged behind. The one parent female subjects scored higher on educational and religious ideas and the other group on family and economic ideals. All the three groups showed singnificant differences on the basis of sex and adjustment.

The study of Srivastava (1982) showed that very few students of the tribal population (8.0 per cent) were in high schools and intermediate colleges. The most pressing problem areas for the tribal students were psychological personal relations (PPR), health and physical development (HPD) and courtship, sex and marriage (CSM), the least pressing problem areas were curriculum and teaching procedure (CTP), adjustment to school work (ASW) and moral and religion (MR). Among the backward caste students the most actue problem areas were courtship, sex and marriage (CSM), health and physical development (HPD) and social and recreational activities (SRA); the least worrying problem areas for this group were home and family (HF), curriculum and teaching procedure (CTP) and adjustment to school work (ASW). In the upper caste student sample, health and physical development (HPD), finances, living conditions and employment (FLE) and social and recreational activities (SRA) problem areas topped the list whereas curriculum and teaching procedure (CTP), further vocation and education (FVE) and personal psychological relations (PPR) were the least worrying problem areas. There was no significant difference in the problems faced by the scheduled tribe students and the upper caste students. The backward caste students had significantly less problems in the area of finance, living conditions and employment. Similarly, they were significantly less worried about the problem area of home and family (HF) than the upper caste students. Irrespective of caste and creed, the students of Mirzapur in general showed a very narrow range of awareness of the world of work. They could name only fourteen occupations for which they aspired. The most aspired for occupations for the tribal students were service (27.3 per cent), teaching (17.5 per cent), engineering (14.8 per cent) or medicine (10.81 per cent). The least aspired for jobs were those of the overseer, magistrate, minister and contractor. The percentage of the tribal students who were uncertain about their occupational aspiration was 13.51 and they did not mention any occupation in the questionnaire. There was no significant difference in the occupational aspiration of the scheduled tribe, the backward class and the upper caste students. There was no significant difference between the scheduled tribe students and the upper caste students in their value orientation. The backward caste students were significantly lower in social values than the upper caste and the scheduled tribe students. The backward caste students were significantly higher on knowledge values than the upper caste students but there was no significant differences between them and the tribal students on the value. The backward caste students were significantly higher on the hedonistic value than the upper caste and the tribal students. The backward caste students were significantly higher on power value than the upper caste and the tribal students. In the hierarchy of values among the tribal students, democratic, social and health values topped the list whereas aesthetic power and hedonistic values were at the bottom.

Democratic, health and social values were at the top of the hierarchy among the upper caste students whereas hedonistic power and aesthetic values were at the bottom. Irrespective of caste and creed, democratic and health values were the two top ranking values.

A study entitled "A study of social, religious and moral values of students of calss XI and their relationship with moral character traits and personality adjustment" by Zamen (1982) revealed that among both the urban and rural samples, raligious values were the strongest, followed by moral values; the social values were the weakest. However the coefficients of correlation between the three values were positive and highly significant. The means of the three values for the students of the rural area were consistently higher than those for the urban area, both in the case of boys and girls. The means of all the three values for the girls were higher than those for boys. Community wise the means for all the three values for the Hindu group were generally higher than those for the Christian or the Muslim groups. All the three values had the greatest influence on character traits and lowest on personality adjustments. In the case of personality adjustment, social values had the greatest influence, followed by moral values. In the case of personality traits included in the study the influence of all the three values, although positive were not found to be uniform. It was found that social and moral values influenced the personality traits much more than religious values. All the five character traits (geniality, helpfulness, kindheartedness, truthfulness, and dutifulness) appeared to be positively and significantly influenced by values. Although this influence was generally uniformly positive on the various groups of the sample, the boys specially of the urban area appeared to be more influenced than the girls.

Diwedi (1983) reported that the place of residence (rural/urban) had a close relationship with values religious, ethico-cultural, political and educational. Age group of the respondents was significantly related with religious, societal, political, economic and educational values. Women were more religious, ethical, cultured, and keenly interested in societal problems compared to men. Scores of men were higher on political values than those of women. Thus, sex played an important role in the development of values. The old values were not shared by the modern youth. They were rather sceptical concerning religion. Widow and intercaste marriages, love marriages, casteless society etc., were popular values of the student respondents. Devaluation in the personality, knowledge and character of the political leaders as well as the teachers of the day was revealed. The traditional, caste-wise occupational structure was no longer liked by the students. Students favoured change in the old curriculum of education as to them, it was useless. They liked co-education and opposed traditional systems of education. They demanded students participation in academic and administrative decision of educational institutions.

Goswami (1983) came to the conclusions that :

(i) The mean differences of scores of theoretical, social and religious values between the teachers of post-basic schools and teachers of ordinary schools were highly significant and were in favour of teachers of post-basic schools. Theoretical, social and religious values of teachers of post basic schools were better than those of teachers of ordinary schools.

(ii) The mean differences of scores of economic, aesthetic and political values between the teachers of post basic schools and teachers of ordinary schools were highly significant and the differences were in favour of teachers of ordinary schools. The economic, aesthetic and political values of teachers of ordinary schools were better than those of teachers of post-basic schools.

(iii) The theoretical, social and religious values of girls studying in post-basic schools were better than the values of girls studying in ordinary schools.

(iv) The economic and aesthetic values of girls studying in ordinary schools were better than those of girls studying in post basic schools. The mean difference of political values of girls was not significant.

(v) The mean differences of score of theoretical social and religious values were significant and were in favour of boys studying in post basic schools.

(vi) The mean differences of scores on economic aesthetic and political values were significant and were in favour of boys studying in ordinary schools.

(vii) The post basic schools provided a better atmosphere in school to inculcate moral, social and religious values and Gandhian thoughts of self-reliance and cleanliness among students than ordinary schools. The students of post basic schools were better in these values and Gandhian thought than students of ordinary schools.

Patni (1983) found that the girls studying in different faculties had almost similar value patterns. All students showed the highest preference for aesthetic values. The girls of all faculties showed comparatively high preference for money and materialistic values over other values. The students showed minimum preference for moral values. The science and commerce students did not differ significantly on aesthetic values but the arts students gave more importance to the aesthetic values. Arts and commerce students had equal knowledge values but the science students gave less importance to knowledge value. Religious values received equal preference from all the three groups. The arts and commerce girls differed significantly on aesthetic values, money and materialistic values and moral values. The science and commerce students differed significantly on knowledge values, social values, national and political values and self values. The arts and science students differed significantly on knowledge values aesthetic values, social values, national and political values, moral values and self values. The science students were found higher on social values and national and political values than the other two groups. The high achievement motivated group put money and material values first and aesthetic values second. In the low-achievement motivated group, the order was reversed. The high achievement motivated girls preferred national and political values over self values whereas the low-achievement motivated girls preferred self values over national and political values. The high and low achievement motivated groups placed the moral values in lowest preference. The high achievement motivated group and the low-achievement motivated group differed significantly on aesthetic values, religious values, national and political values and moral values. The low achievement motivated group was more aesthetic and more religious than the high achievement motivated group. These two groups, with high and low-achievement motivation, did not differ significantly on knowledge values money and material values, social values and self values. The correlations of values and achievement motivation of each category of values in all the three groups were found to be insignificant. In the group of arts students knowledge values, aesthetic values and money and material values were negatively correlated with level of achievement motivation, whereas in the science group only knowledge and aesthetic values, and in the commerce group, only money and material values were negatively correlated with the level of achievement of these students. In the science group the money and material values, religious values, social values, national political self and moral values, correlated positively with the achievement motivation level of the students, but the correlation was insignificant. The girls of the commerce faculty had positive though insignificant correlation of achievement motivation with the all categories of values except money material values. Religious values, social national political values self values and moral values had the positive but insignificant correlation with achievement motivation.

Pratap and Srivastav (1983) made an attempt to study the need pattern of values of technical persons belonging to various economic groups. The study reported that the upper class technical persons were significantly higher on aesthetic values than the middle class ones. There was statistically significant difference between middle and lower class technical persons in theoretical and political values. The middle class persons were higher on theoretical values while the lower class persons were higher on political values. There was statistically significant difference between upper and lower class technical persons in the value areas of social, political and religious. The upper class persons held high social values than the lower class ones while the lower class persons held high political and religious value than their upper class counterparts.

In his study Annamma (1984) concluded that a majority of the college students were conformists, with a stable system of values, and without rebellious tendencies. The younger college students were more spiritualism oriented as compared to the older group which was more materialism oriented. Academic achievement, residential backgrounds and father's education and occupational status had no relationship to value orientation of college students. Economic status was related to value orientation with the lower income group being more spiritualism oriented and the higher income group more materialism oriented. Size of family was related to value orientation with students from large families being more spiritualism oriented and those from small size families more materialism oriented. A majority of students did not have clear goals about education, occupation or marriage. Male students exhibited higher aspiration than female students. No discrepancies were seen between self and parental aspirations. Marriage was not viewed as an immediate prospect. Boys and girls approved intermingling, but girls were seen to prefer the customary type of marriage. Female students were seen to be better adjusted than male students in all the areas studied college education was not seen to have any impact on value orientation and the behaviour of the students.

In this work Bhatnagar (1984) concluded that the size of the family affected student activism, adjustment and values. Students belonging to small families had less activistic tendencies, better adjustment, higher values (educational, personal and material and better school learning). Religious, social and humanistic values were not found to be significantly related with the size of the family. Birth order was found to be related with activism, adjustment and personal, educational, social and materialistic values, while religious and humanistic values were not found to be related with birth order. Socioeconomic status was found to be significantly related with activism, educational and materialistic values, and school learning, whereas it was not found to be related with personal, religious and humanistic values. The broken family was positively related to activism, poor adjustment, and high personal and materialistic values, while the intact family was positively related to educational and social values.

Another interesting study was conducted by Sawhney (1984). He compared delinquents and non-delinquents boys in relation to personality adjustment and values. The findings of the study were :

(i) The delinquents showed significant differences from non-delinquents in respect of extroversion/introversion. Social maladjustment and automism and denial.

(ii) The delinquents showed significantly poor adjustment on home health, emotional, social and total adjustment.

(iii) As regards values the delinquents differed in their preference of values as compared to non-delinquents marked differences were observed on values of Broadminded; 'Capable'; 'Clean'; 'Forgiving'; 'Honest'; 'Obedient'; 'Responsible' and self controlled on case of delinquents.

Sawhney (1984) revealed that the distribution of scores of both boys and girls of TDC and PUC in all eight values deviated from the normal. The PUC boys exhibited significantly higher mean values in health and aesthetic values than TDC boys. TDC girls showed higher mean scores than boys in social and aesthetic values. The high-intelligent boys of PUC exhibited significantly higher mean scores than the high intelligent girls of PUC in social, political, economic values. The low-intelligent boys of PUC exhibited significantly lower mean scores than the low intelligent PUC girls in social political, economic and recreation values. The high intelligent girls of TDC showed significant differences in social, moral, knowledge and aesthetic values than the TDC high-intelligent boys. The low-intelligent girls of TDC attached more importance to knowledge value than boys. PUC boys of his SES exhibited higher mean values than PUC girls of high SES in social and recreation values. PUC boys of high SES showed higher mean scores in recreation values than girls of high SES TDC girls of high SES showed a significant difference in social, economic, moral and knowledge values than the low SES boys of TDC. Two dominant factor loudings emerged for all the four groups. In case of PUC boys the factors were, 'Aesthetic Recreation factor' and 'Politics-economic factors'. In case of PUC girls the first and second factors were 'moral-cum-knowledge factor' and 'Aesthetic creation factor'. In case of TDC boys two factors extracted were 'political-cum-knowledge factor' and 'Aesthetic-Recreation Factor'. In case of TDC girls the two factors were 'moral-cum-knowledge factors' and 'Aesthetic-Recreation factor'.

Parmar (1986) undertook a sociological analysis of social values and aspirations of youth in a changing rural environment. The sample consisted of 296 male and 54 female students who were selected using the stratified random sampling technique, from all the six rural colleges of Pratapgarh district affiliated to Avadh university. The main findings of the study were :

I. Acquisition of knowledge was the main aim of education according to the majority of students. More than half favoured vocational-technical education.

II. A sizeable number of students wanted education for females and believed its purpose was to make them self-dependent.

III. Students planned to continue their studies further. Most of them studied arts subjects. Their educational aspiration was of medium level.

IV. There seemed to be a close relationship between educational aspiration and social class, caste and sex.

V. The ideal profession was considered to be that which gave status in society and developed personality. Teaching was considered as an ideal profession. Higher administrative services and agriculture occupied second and third places.

VI. For success in one's profession health family background and behaviour were considered as significant factors.

VII. Students were mostly inclined to seek white-collar jobs. They were determined to achieve their professional aspirations and wanted to join these professions because of personal interest, higher income and status.

VIII. Aspiration for material objects was limited income aspiration was also low.

IX. Social mobility was limited.

X. A positive relationship seemed to exist between social class, caste and sex and aspirations for profession material possessions and income.

XI. About two-thirds of the students were interested in politics. A good number of them considered it a form of national service. Their political ideology resembled that of the congress (I) party.

XII. Student union elects were generally disfavoured reduction in the age of franchise was desired. The democratic form of government was liked by most students and unemployment was considered as the greatest problem of the country.

XIII. There was a relative relationship between social class caste and sex and interest in politics.

Paul (1986) found that the urban adolescents were more highly oriented to competence. Maturity and maintaining harmonious relations; more affectionately disposed to others, with sincerity and tolerance; and strove for the accomplishment of their goal in more mature and competent ways than rural adolescents. They had a stronger social orientation than rural adolescents. The rural adolescents were more concerned about economic returns and variety, whereas the urban adolescents were more concerned about prestige. The college adolescents were more strongly oriented towards applying themselves steadily to goals aimed at more stable and more optimistic, whereas school adolescents were more oriented to appreciating the value of tidiness with respect to social values, the college adolescents strive more social harmony peace and social service, while the school adolescents were more oriented to showing warm affection to others. The college adolescents were more courageous while the school adolescents were more oriented towards being independent and loving to others. In the case of terminal values, the school adolescents were more strongly oriented towards enjoying happiness and social recognition. While college adolescents strived more for freedom and mature appreciation. With respect to work values, the school adolescents strived more for economic returns and intellectual stimulation, whereas college adolescents strived more towards achievement orientation. The male adolescents were more striving for their ambition and excellence and more service-oriented than female adolescents. The female adolescents were more oriented to appreciating tidiness more aesthetic in nature, conscious of being punctual and regular. More striving for harmony, love, sympathy tolerance, peace and more oriented to competence and sound character, striving more for happiness, a peaceful life and gaining economic returns, as compared to male adolescents. The science-stream adolescents strived more for strong work habits and were more courageous than general stream adolescents. Their orientation was more towards maintaining and practising social relation in comparison with the general stream adolescents. The science stream adolescents were more competence oriented, strived more for freedom and recognition as compared to general-stream students who strived for happiness and comfort. The general-stream students strived more towards seeking a job full of variety and society and social contact than the science-stream students. Factor analysis showed rural adolescents striving for personal happiness and competence, having a materialistic best of mind, striving for self-discipline, more concerned about prestige and economic returns, attaching importance to dignity of work, striving for national security, being more service-oriented, striving for self-esteem-orientation, gaining self-strength and showing signs of social and personal retardation. The factors underlying the value-orientation of urban adolescents were the striving for pleasure and security, creative achievement, self-constricted personality, personal courage, social orientation, self-adaptation, low achievement-orientation a strong learning towards working more earnestly for achievement of their aspirations, being more moralistics seeking recognition pleasure, social harmony, more concerned about self-reliance.

The study of Rizvi (1986) showed that a majority of students held moderate attitudes towards religious education, but the students of the Hindu and Muslim religious groups were found to hold different attitudes towards religious education. Favourable attitudes towards religious education were found to be associated with such values as helpfulness, preserving traditions and adaptation to nature. In this respect sex, socio-economic status and religious group differences were not found. Irrespective of the differences in their sex, socio-economic status, and religion, students held similar views with respect to the association between attitudes towards religious education and conservative liberal and scientific fatalistic value dimension.

Singh (1986) made a comparative study of values (economic, social, political, theoretical, religious, moral and aesthetic) problems (academic, financial and social) and level of frustration (aggression, fixation, resignation and regression) among Harijan and non-Harijan undergraduate students of Bhagalpur University. In all 300 harijan and 200 non-Harijan male undergraduate students comparable in age, sex, education and socio-economic status of their parents were selected from three degree colleges located at Banka, Godda and Sahileganj of Bhagalpur University. He concluded that Harijan students were significantly higher on economic and religious values and lower on social political, theoretical, moral and aesthetic values. They had significantly more frequent and intense academic, financial and social problems in comparison with non-Harijan students. Non-Harijans were significantly more aggressivge than Harijan students. There was no significant difference in the regressive behaviour of harijan and non-Harijan students. Harijan displayed more fixated and resignated behaviour than non-Harijan students.

Manav (1988) conducted a study on attitudes, self-concept and values of professional and non-professional college students in relation to achievement. The sample consisted of 116 final year engineering students. From Roorke University 100 M.B.B.S. students, 151 B.Ed. students and 523 final year mere graduates students (B.A. and B.Sc.) of affiliated colleges of Meerut University. The major findings of the study were : (i) there was significant difference between professional and non-professional students with regard to their self-concept, attitudes and values (ii) the professional college students emerged as person who perceived themselves to be more confident and higher achievers than the non-professional students (iii) the professional students had dominant personal and humanistic values, while non-professional students had more religious values (iv) the non-professional students had more positive attitude towards their teachers and society than professional students (v) significant differences existed between engineering medical and teacher training students on majority of the values, attitudes and self-concept (vi) the engineering and medical students possessed higher personal, materialistic and educational values the student teachers (vii) the student-teachers were found to be more religious and humanistic the medical and engineering students, and (viii) there was no significant relationship between the students self-concept and achievement between students attitude and achievement and between students' values and achievement.

Mishra (1991) carried out a study on certain sociological background variables of values in high school students. The objectives of the study were : (i) to study the value patterns of students of grade-IX (ii) to determine whether the sociological background variables (*i.e.* SES, mother's level of education, caste and birth order) has a bearing on value patterns of students and (iii) to differentiate the values of male and female students. The following were the findings (i) in total personal values boys had high personal values than the girls (ii) 'hedonistic value' was the most preferred value for the total sample and the 'aesthetic value' the least one (iii) the boys preferred most the 'power value' and the least 'aesthetic value' while for the girls most preferred value was 'hedonistic value' and the least was 'aesthetic value', (iv) the socio-economic status of further did not influence the personal value of the students (v) the mother's level of education is not significantly associated with the personal value of students (vi) the association between caste and the personal value is found to be insignificant (vii) birth order has no influence. On the personal value of students, (viii) there is no sex difference in total personal value but in the value areas like social and power boys do differ from girls. In both the personal value areas (*i.e.* social and power) boys had high personal value than the girls.

Sanyal (1991) conducted a study to see if there was any reflection of science education on value profile particularly in respect of two significant levels of science education (*i.e.* post-graduate and undergraduate). The Indian version of All Port—vernon-Lindzey's study of values (1958) was used to assess the values of the participants in this study. The sample of the study consisted of 194 science male students (*i.e.* 121 post-graduate and 73 undergraduates) of Calcutta university.

He found that both the post graduate and undergraduate male science students preferred the theoretical value most and the religious value least. There was slight differences in the similarity in ranks of other values. There was significant differences between the post-graduates and undergraduates in economic and social values. There was greater preference for economic value among the undergraduate science male students and greater amount of likings for social values among the post-graduate science male students.

In this study Das (1993) investigated the value profiles of science, arts and commerce higher secondary students. The findings of the study were (i) The student belonging to arts stream had highest preference for 'religious values' and least preference for 'aesthetic value'. (ii) 'Power' and 'family prestige' were equally most preferred values for science students and 'aesthetic value' was the least one. (iii) The most preferred value for the commerce student was 'economic value' and the least one was 'democratic value' (iv) Boys preferred the most to the power value and the least to the 'aesthetic value' (v) The most and least preferred values for girls were 'family prestige' and 'aesthetic' respectively. (vi) Similarity in rank of 'economic' and 'knowledge' values was noticed for boys and girls (vii) The students belonging to Arts and Science streams resemble in ranking of 'hedonistic' and 'health' values. (viii) Significant resemblances exist between arts and science students regarding religious, social aesthetic, knowledge, hedonistic power, family prestige and health values. (ix) Democratic and economic values were the areas of value where arts and science students differed significantly in their value preferences. (x) Significance of differences of value between arts and commerce were found in the areas of social democratic, aesthetic economic knowledge hedonistic power and family prestige. (xi) In the value areas of social, democratic aesthetic, economic, knowledge, hedonistic, and power and in total values, science and commerce students differ significantly. (xii) Significant sex differences were found in the five value areas like religious, democratic, hedonistic power and family prestige. In religious democratic and family prestige value areas, girls had high personal values than the boys and the boys had more preference for hedonistic and power values.

Tewari and Tewari (1993) conducted a study with the purpose of investigating the differences in the value patterns of high and low caste male students. The major findings were (i) Significant caste differences were found only in theoretical aesthetic and religious areas. (ii) High caste students were found more interested in the discovery of truth, artistic aspects of life, mystical and sought to comprehend the cosmos as a whole to relate himself to its embracing totality.

Verma, Das and Swain (1993) explored values of adolescent students as a function of their sex and rural urban inhabitation. A sample of 300 students of grade X of four randomly selected high schools of Cuttack (Orissa) was drawn by cluster random sampling technique. The value inventory standardised by Sambhi (1988) was used to collect on the values of adolescent students. They found that the main effect of sex has been found to be significant in case of truth, non-violence and love values. The male students had higher level of truth, non-violence and love values than female students. The main effect of inhabitation was observed in the means of truth, non-violence, right conducted, love and peace values. The rural adolescent students had higher value of truth, non-violence, right conduct, love and peace as compared to their urban counterparts. The interaction between sex and inhabitation was found to be significant in case of truth and love values. The male adolescent students tended to have higher level of truth value in urban group than female adolescent students. Further, rural inhabitation exhibited higher level of love value than urban inhabitation in male group but not in female group.

Chandrakumar and Arockiaswamy (1994) conducted a study to explore the value system of the first degree college students and to study the extent of the influence of the college climate and home climate over the value system and the extent of the influence of the value system over the personality characteristics. For this purpose they took a sample of 1050 students of the first degree arts and science from colleges affiliated to Madurai Kamaraj University. The major findings were :

(i) The first degree college students gave much importance to social values such as loving and equality, personal values such as freedom, honesty, happiness and competence, (ii) The value system did not have significant relationship with the personality dimensions of the sampled students. (iii) Neither the college climate nor the home climate was related to the value system of the first degree college students.

The study of Narayanan *et al.* (1994) was planned to determine the possible differences in value of orientation among male and female college students. A random sampling technique was used to select a sample of 120 male and 150 female college students in Coimbatore. The value orientation scale developed by Natrajan (1980) was used to measure the values held by individuals. The results revealed that the male students considered 12 values to be important and feel committed to them. The values include the terminal values of love and instrumental values of self-respect, power, wealth, status, progress, education, ambition, aspiration, work, capability, self-control and accomplishment. The female students considered 13 values to be important and feel committed to them. The values include the terminal values of truth, devotion to God, equality, morality, honesty, friendship and helpfulness and the instrumental values of power, individuality, duty, security, education and self-control.

The male students considered certain values to be not important and do not feel committed to them. These include the terminal values of truth, non-violence, devotion to God, culture, equality, conscience, humour, beauty, rationality, peace and salvation and the instrumental values of health, language, children, caste, marriage, life, relatives, duty, security, creativity and country. The female students considered the values including the terminal values of beauty, rationality, peace, salvation and wisdom and the instrumental values of self-respect, language, status, children, caste, marriage, live, relative, politics, work, sports and self control to be not important and do not feel committed to them.

The male students considered certain values to be important but do not feel committed to them. These include the terminal values of morality, honesty, character, and obedience and the instrumental values of family, individuality, law and religion. The female students consider such values including the terminal values of conscience, humour culture and character and the instrumental values of wealth, family, health, law, progress, ambition, creativity, aspiration capability and country as important but do not feel committed to them.

The male students considered certain values to be not important but feel committed to them. These include the terminal values of wisdom, friendship, and helpfulness and the instrumental values of politics, freedom and sports. The female students consider such values including the terminal values of non-violence, love and obedience and the instumental values of accomplishment, freedom and religious to be not important but feel committed to them.

The findings revealed interesting differences between the patterns of values of the male and female students. The male attribute importance to the values including status, progress and accomplishment than the females. The females attribute importance to the values including, truth, self-respect, power, non-violence, health, language, devotion to God, culture, equality, conscience, marriage, duty, life, security, ambition, creativity, rationality, peace, friendship, helpfulness, and self-confidence than the males.

The males show higher commitment than the females to the following values, power, aspiration, progress, sports. The females on the other hand show higher commitment than the males to values such as self-respect, truth, non-violence, family, health, children, devotion to God, equality, conscience, marriage, beauty, life, law, humour, creativity, morality, honesty, character, friendship, obedience and helpfulness.

Nayak (1994) studied value variations in the ninth and twelth grade students. The investigation was conducted with a view to :

(i) Compare the values between ninth grade and twelth grade students to see the effect of age,

(ii) To compare the values between boys and grils to see the effect of sex,

(iii) To compare the values of students with respect to place of residence. The sample for the study was drawn from four high schools and four junior colleges of Ganjam district (Orissa). The sample comprised 150 students (*i.e.* 75 IX grades and 75 XII graders). The personal value questionnaire (PVQ) by Sherry and Verma (1978) was used to measure the values of students. The findings of the study were : (i) in the value areas like religious, social, democratic, aesthetic, knowledge, health and total value the twelfth grades have excelled their ninth grader counter parts. (ii) significant sex differences were found in the three value areas like religious, social, knowledge and in total value. In "religious" and "knowledge" value areas boys had high personal values than girls and the girls had more preference for "social" values. (iii) significance of differences of values between urban and rural area students were found in the areas of religious, aesthetic, power and in total personal values. The urban areas students were found to have more religious, aesthetic and power values. (iv) "Religious" values was the single value area where the students whether categorised into boys or girls or into urban and rural or into ninth grades and twelfth graders differed significantly. (v) The boys belonging to class IX were more religious and more knowledgeable than their girls counter parts while girls were more sociable. (vi) The ninth graders coming from urban areas were more religious and more knowledgeable than their rural counter parts. (vii) "Power" was the only area of value where the twelfth grade boys differed significantly from their girls counter parts. However, the difference goes in favour of boys. (viii) In the value areas like religious social, aesthetic and power the rural urban difference was noted for twelfth graders. The urban area students (*i.e.* class XII) had more preference for religious, aesthetic and power values while the rural area students preferred most the social values.

An attempt was made by Chandrakumar and Arockiasamy (1997) to study the gender difference in the value orientation among the college students. It was found that the female students had little better value orientation than the male students. The mean score for all the items for the female students was little higher than the male students. Both the male and female groups had shown a very moderate preference for certain values. Gender did not influence the value orientation of the college students. The values preferred by both the male and female students mainly were love ambition and honesty. There was no consistency in the preference and values by the students in all three years.

Singh (1997) studied the values of urban and rural adolescent students of Aligarh and found that in the theoretical and religious values urban male and female adolescents had significantly higher meaning scores than the corresponding mean scores of rural male and female adolescents. In Social and Aesthetic values rural male and female adolescents had significantly higher mean scores. In Political and Economic values the mean difference of urban and rural adolescents were not significant. The male adolescent students had got significantly higher mean score than those of female adolescents in Theoretical and Economic values which were due to the influence of culture and society where male adolescents had better opportunity for their education. In other two values *viz* social and political, female adolescents had higher mean scores than male adolescents.

The study of Verma et al. (1998) was designed to study whether SCs and non-SCs students differed significantly with regard to their personal value. The sample of the study comprised 120 students studying in class xii in four senior secondary schools of district Sirsa (Haryana). The tools used to collect the data were PVQ by Sherry and Verma. The collected data were treated with mean, SD and t' test. The major findings were :

(i) Non-SCs male students had significantly more inclination towards economic, hedonistic, power and family prestige.

(ii) Non-Scheduled Caste female students received significantly more mean score on aesthetic, economic, knowledge, hedonistic power and health values than Scheduled Castes female students.

(iii) Among the Scheduled Caste male students had more Social and Knowledge values, and female students possessed more family prestige value.

(iv) Among the Non-Scheduled Caste, females had greater mean score on religious, aesthetic and knowledge values as compared to male students.

IMPLICATION OF PREVIOUS RESEARCH FOR THE PRESENT STUDY

From the review of the research studies, it is quite apparent that values in the context of academic achievement of higher secondary students have not been touched either abroad or in Indian context. Value patterns which seem to be an important factor in the learning process (Cattell, Sealey and Sweney, 1966) needs to be studied in relation to the academic performance of the students who prepare themselves for entering into higher education. Some of the foreign studies (Dewinter, 1961; Thomson, 1961; Cole and Miller, 1967; Walker, 1970; Hapner, Mulder, 1974) attempted to find out the relationship between values and achievement. Most of the these studies were based on the samples of teachers trainees, trainees in the nursing training programmes or on some kind of professional groups. However, in those studies academic achievement was significantly related to the values of students.

In India, very little efforts have been made to study values in relation to academic achievement of students at higher secondary level. Most of the studies are on the students of higher education or professional education or athletes. The study of Rajput (1985) is the only case in which attempts were made to study values across the academic streams (*i.e.* faculty differences). Most of the Indian studies were of comparative types.

In the present study, therefore, the researcher studied the value patterns of higher secondary school students belonging to different academic streams in relation to their achievement.

4
CONTEXT OF THE STUDY

RATIONALE OF THE STUDY

Human beings of the present era are enthralled with the advancement of science as well as encountering the several complexities which are the ultimate by products of any scientific progression. There is concern for behavioural stability amidst the changing social systems. The need for behavioural reorientation to match the current trends of the world is also felt. Mankind has been constantly striving for emancipation, *i.e.* freedom to choose its own destiny. During its long and chequered history mankind has developed three forces to control its group destiny *viz* social, political and economic and evolved some sort of value system to provide life and blood to the individual and society. Every known society has a value system a set of rules and goals that guide its conduct and judgements. The business of social life proceeds on the assumption that the values established in the groups are the ones that must be respected and enforced. With this end in view, every cultured society has developed some educational system to operate within its socio-economic and political system because education is one of the potent factors most likely to influence and modify ones behaviour. The social scientists (Rokeach, 1973; Schiffman and Kanuk, 1983; and Korper *et al* 1986) have kept their faith on 'value' approach either to induce change in behaviour or to gauge the stable value systems in the individuals personality framework.

From the above discussion, it is apparent that the search for a sound philosophy that can sustain the human race in this 'nuclear age' is but 'Spirituality' and this spirituality is what is missing today with all the advances in science and technology, there is more conflict and greater misery because spirituality was missing. Further the downward pull of the forces like freedom, adventure, creative imagination, clarity of thinking had sealed the fate of many civilisations in the past and it is threatening to destroy our intellectual and moral fibre today. But fortunately the light-of the mind has not been totally put out all over the world and history is replete with instances of how the mind has devised its own ways of eventually overpowering its captors. Even when harshly harassed for giving expression to their unpopular views or ideas, men of the calibre of socrates, christ, Lincoln, Gandhiji and Radhakrishnan courageous upheld their convictions and the right of man to freedom of though. Galileo was pressured to give up his support to the copernician theory under threat of torture. But even as he was signing the recantation, he is said to have muttered. Thus the great martyrs of history have been those who undauntedly perceived the truth whether in the realm of knowledge or of values and who were ready, when necessary to make the supreme sacrifice.

The quality of life, therefore, can not be enhanced without the unhampered pilgrimage of the mind towards truth and excellence which constitute the power house of creativity and the spring-board for all human values, our educational institutions will have to stress the significance of thought and moral values because as the late Prof. Saiyidain (1962) tellingly remarks "Without the saving grace of free end swift thought, man would be reduced to the level of a mere pigmy a speck of dust dancing helplessly in the wind for a brief meaningless second on one of the smallest of the innumerable planets". Higher creative life is the clearest and purest expression of the essential characteristic of the life at all its points and levels. All life however commonplace, is saturated with the selfsame elements whose infloresence is literature, philosophy, science, arts and religion. They proclaim the victory of the creative human spirit striving towards more truth, more goodness, more beauty, more light. But modern education that different educational institutions are expected to impart, has to adress itself to the lofty tasks of emancipating man's mind from the stranglehold of conservatism and obscurantism. Vivekananda (1932) condemns man's reactionary tendency to seek asylum in the moth-eaten traditions of his forefathers and invest them with an unjustified sanctity. Man's true life as Russell (1940) has aptly argued, consists not in the satisfaction of his pressing physical wants but "in art and thought and love, in the creation and contemplation of beauty and in the scientific understanding of the world".

The greatest need of today is that man in his mad race in pursuit of transient materialistic gains and objectives, should at least occasionally, pause and reflect on the real purpose and value of human life and give a fresh orientation to his view of his life based on such introspective reflection. If this were done one should have no difficulty to realise that amongst all living species the human being occupies a special and exalted place by reason of his alone being endowed with powers of reason and discrimination aided by a discerning intellect and faculties of analytical thinking, assimilation and recollection. From time immemorial these special gifts have generated in man a keen sense of inquiry in search of truth, wisdom and bliss.

The most precious asset possessed by our country is our glorious ancient culture firmly founded on the principles of 'Sanathana Dharma'. This culture has been handed down from generation to generation during the past thousands of years and it lies embedded in the hearts and souls of the millions of our people belonging to different religious faiths who are knit together by this common cultural bond unless the training given to our children is such as to acquaint them with the fundamentals of the glorious ancient culture of India and develop in their minds a deep and abiding respect for all faiths as well as a keen sense of pride about our unique cultural heritage, the preservation of our cultural heritage will be seriously imperilled.

Under the educational system which is currently in vogue in our country the emphasis is solely on the imparting of knowledge concerning the academic subjects included in the curriculum, and least attention is usually paid to the development of the childs character and inner personality. The result is that children grow up without getting any opportunity to know about glorious cultural traditions of our country and the great moral and spiritual values on which that culture is based. Student power today is not harnessed collectively for the attainment of social harmony and well-being. The restlessness that has lately polluted the atmosphere of our educational institution is undoubtedly the result of a soul-sickness that has seized the Indian youth on account of their innermost cultural aspirations having remained unheeded. It is only when they are enabled to plunge into the depths of their own souls and pursue the quest of discovering the Divine in each human heart that they will be drawn towards establishing themselves as members of a society based on pure and unselfish love and unstilted mutual co-operation. For this it is absolutely necesary that an opportunity should be provided to the students to acquaint themselves with the basic feature of our glorious spiritual and cultural heritage which, with its essential universality, cuts as under all distinctions of caste, community, race and religion and underlines the brotherhood of man and the fatherhood of God. Such broad, based education will prompt the students to devote every minute of activity of theirs for the pilgrimage to the God within themselves through the path of selfless service to fellowmen. Such an integrated process of correcting and shaping the childs attitudes and reactions will mould them into ideal citizen most useful to the society, befitting our great traditions.

Of all the countries in the world, we in India have the richest cultural and spiritual heritage. But values in the modern world are changing so rapidly that the young find themselves quite bewildered when they try to form their value perspectives or when they try to cherish or choose values. "The rate of change", as Gajjar (1985) writes, "in the context of value is increasing so fast as to cause a shock". Raths *et al.* express the predicaments of the students in the following words:

> ***It seems to us that the pace and complexity of modern life has so exacerbated the problem of deciding what is good and what is right and what is desirable that large number of children are finding it increasingly bewildering, even overwhelming, to decide what is worth valuing, what is worth time an energy.***

In India the whole population in general and the students in particular, due to their inexperience are facing the same problems, because as Thomas (1970) puts it, "the traditional values are weakended and new values are emerging". In this context the Indian Education commission (1964-66) points out:

> ***The old values which held society together are disappearing and as there is no effective programme to replace them by a new sense of social responsibility, innumerable signs of social disorganisation are evident every where and are continually on the increase. These include strikes, increasing lawlessness, and a disregard for public property, corruption in public life and communal tensions and troubles. Student unrest of which so much is written is only one, and is probably a minor one of those symptoms.***

Thus there is the need of a comprehensive programme of value education which can enable students to meet new situations in the world of values, not only as they are now, but also in any new situation that many arise in future.

It is generally noticed that students are lacking in formation of conscious goals of life. As Haq (1985) writes: "their concepts of goals are nebulous, hazy and conflicting ever increasing their emotional disturbances and rendering them more and more unhappy". Clear and convincing goals give zest a well as meaning to life. A programme of education in values can definitely help students in this regard. This certainly demands an involvement's in different values, not in morality alone.

When one comes to the issue of mental health which is so badly lacking among many in the modern world one comes to know, as Gajjar (1985) does on the basis of studies that "besides physiological, biochemical, social, cultural and human relationship factors affective experiences and other needs and purposes of the individuals inner life are of importance."This necessitates a programme of value education which make the students aware of their inner lives, and train them how to synthesize the needs and purpose of the inner lives with those of the outer.

The time has come to act the call now is, Do leap into the branch and save the world. All this rests on our educational institutions to harness the inner potentials of their students and channelise them in such a way that their intellectual pursuits promote and strengthen appropriate attitudes, respect of the diversity cultures and the dignity and freedom of the individual and adopt traditional values to the new conditions and needs that are evolving.

It is clear from the above discussion that value system plays an important role in the decision making process. In fact every human action is the reflection of personal or social values. The present situation of India calls for a system of education which apart from strengthening national unity must strengthen social solidarity through meaningful and constructive value education. Before launching any comprehensive educational programme to promote students' personal values, it is essential to study the prevalent value system held by the students. Thus, the present study is an humble attempt in that direction. More specifically, the problem of the study may be stated as follows:

> ***A study of value profiles of students of Science, Arts and Commerce at the Higher Secondary Level of Education in relation to their Academic Achievement***

ASSUMPTIONS

While attempting to assess values of students and looking for the factors associated with it, the investigator has been guided by the relevant literature to base the present piece of research on the following assumptions.

(i) The values of students is a significant area of study, although neglected so far in educational research.
(ii) Values of students are quantifiable and happen to be a function of several psychological factors of which academic achievement is one of them.
(iii) Having studied the factors, mainly the achievement, associated with values of students, steps could be taken up to enhance it so that the deterioration of values be checked.
(iv) Students with positive values are the assets of the society.

OBJECTIVES OF THE STUDY

On the basis of the statement of the problem, the study aimed at achieving the following objectives:

(i) To determine the value profiles of the higher secondary students across their academic streams (*i.e.* science, arts and commerce), residential background (*i.e.* rural and urban), sex (male and female), and achievement level (*i.e.* high achievers and low achievers).
(ii) To compare the value patterns of higher secondary students belonging to different academic streams (*i.e.* Science, Arts and Commerce).
(iii) To compare the values of higher secondary rural and urban students across their academic streams.
(iv) To compare the values of higher secondary male and female students across their academic streams.
(v) To compare the values of high and low achievers, at the higher secondary level of education, across their academic streams.

HYPOTHESES

Keeping in view the above objectives, the following hypotheses were formulated and tested under present study.

(i) The higher secondary students will have differential value profiles in terms of their academic streams, residential background, sex and achievement level.
(ii) Value patterns of students as represented by three different academic streams (*i.e.* Science, Arts and Commerce) of higher secondary education will be significantly different.
(iii) There will be significant difference in the values of:
    a) Rural and Urban students.
    b) Arts Rural and Science Rural students.

c) Science Rural and Commerce Rural students.
d) Arts Rural and Commerce Rural students.
e) Arts Urban and Science Urban students.
f) Science Urban and Commerce Urban students.
g) Arts Urban and Commerce Urban students.
h) Science Urban and Science Rural students.
i) Arts Urban and Arts Rural students.
j) Commerce Urban and Commerce Rural students.
k) Science Urban and Arts Rural students.
l) Science Urban and Commerce Rural students.
m) Arts Urban and Science Rural students.
n) Arts Urban and Commerce Rural students.
o) Commerce Urban and Science Rural students, and
p) Commerce Urban and Arts Rural students.

(iv) There will be significant difference in the values of:
a) Male and Female students.
b) Arts Male and Science Male Students.
c) Science Male and Commerce Male students.
d) Arts Male and Commerce Male students.
e) Arts Female and Science Female students.
f) Science Female and Commerce Female students.
g) Arts Female and Commerce Female students.
h) Science Male and Science Female students.
i) Arts Male and Arts Female students.
j) Commerce Male and Commerce Female students.
k) Science Male and Arts Female students.
l) Science Male and Commerce Female students.
m) Commerce Male and Commerce Female students.
n) Science Male and Arts Female students.
o) Science Male and Commerce Female students.
p) Arts Male and Science Female students.
q) Arts Male and Commerce Female students.
r) Commerce Male and Science Female students.
s) Commerce Male and Arts Female students.

(v) There will be significant difference in the values of:
a) High Achievers and Low Achievers.
b) High Achievers of Science and Arts Streams.
c) High Achievers of Science and Commerce Streams.
d) High Achievers of Arts and Commerce Streams.
e) Low Achievers of Science Stream and Low Achievers of Arts Stream.

f) Low Achievers of Science Stream and Low Achievers of Commerce Stream.
g) Low Achievers of Arts Stream and Low Achievers of Commerce Stream.
h) High and Low Achievers of Science Stream.
i) High and Low Achievers of Arts Stream.
j) High and Low Achievers of Commerce Stream.
k) High Achievers of Science Stream and Low Achievers of Arts Stream.
l) High Achievers of Science Stream and Low Achievers of Commerce Stream.
m) High Achievers of Arts Stream and Low Achievers of Science Stream.
n) High Achievers of Arts Stream and Low Achievers of Commerce Stream.
o) High Achievers of Commerce Stream and Low Achievers of Science Stream.
p) High Achievers of Commerce Stream and Low Achievers of Arts Stream.

OPERATIONAL DEFINITIONS OF THE KEY TERMS USED

The Key terms which have been used in the title of the study are operationally defined here.

Value Profiles

Value is a human concept. Persons value experiences, states of their being, things, processes etc. and this means that they favour or desire those value is any experience, state, ideal or thing existing or conceived ideally, which is favoured or desired, provided that the experience, state, ideal or thing is justified ends-wise as well as means-wise. Thus, value is that which is desired justifiably. It's justifiability is inbuilt in desirability, then value is that which is desirable.

Value in this study is considered as that "what Sherry and Verma's (1978) Personal value Questionnaire measures".

The word 'profile' has been defined by Harriman (1947) as an arrangement of test scores which indicates the relative standing of an individual on various psychological measures. Good (1959) defines it any graphic technique usually a line diagram, that indicates the relative position of one person or group on each of several tests or other measures. Wolman (1973) considers profile analysis as a procedure used in assessing an individuals uniqueness and trait organisation which consists of establishing pattern of traits in the profile of the individual. Aggarwal and Biswas (1971) define the profile graph as a graph indicating the performance of an individual on a series of tests or a series of ratings of his personality traits.

One common characteristic found in different definitions of a profile refers to the relative standing or position of a person or a group of persons on different aspects. Viewed in this way, the word 'value profile' implies relative standing of higher secondary students belonging to three different academic streams (*i.e.* Science, Arts and Commerce) on ten value areas, namely, religious, social, democratic, aesthetic, economic, knowledge, hedonistic, power, family prestige and health.

Higher Secondary Level of Education

Education, broadly, has three stages, namely primary, secondary and university. The higher secondary stage which covers XI and XII classes comes after secondary stage. This stage is both terminal and preparatory.

In the present study higher secondary level refers to the final year of higher secondary level (*i.e.* class-XII).

Academic Achievement

According to Wiley and Andrew (1955), one of the main purposes of measuring the achievement of pupils is to ascertain the degrees to which the educational objectives of the school are being realised. The results of the measurement of achievement, taken at intervals over a period of years, provide a continuous means of evaluating the students growth and help to determine the effectiveness of the curriculum in meeting the individual needs. The other purposes served by achievement measurements, on the basis of standardised tests, are diagnosis and prediction tests.

According to Baron and Benard (1962), the concept of achievement involves the interaction of three factors, namely, aptitude for learning, readiness for learning and opportunity for learning. Achievement in education, precisely speaking, implies one's knowledge, understanding or skills etc. in a specified subject or a group of subjects.

Generally, teachers use marks to record their judgement about the students level of academic achievement. These marks are generally based on the internal and external examinations. The marks represent estimates of the proficiency possessed by the student in school subjects. Some research studies despite criticism, support the view point that the marks obtained or the academic level attained on the basis of these examinations, continue to be fairly stable.

In the present study, academic achievement is operationally defined as the average percentage of marks obtained by a student in the annual examination of class-XI and mid-sessional examination of class XII conducted by the individual institutions.

DELIMITATIONS

No study is complete in itself and it is bound to have some limitations which depends on resources of the investigator and they are termed as delimitations of the study. Following are the delimitations of the present study.

(i) The study was confined to two major variables (*i.e.* values and academic achievement). Variables selected for the study were related to the two domains, namely affective and cognitive respectively. Their presence in students and their relationship with each other was not an easy task to measure. Further academic achievement was measured in terms of percentage of marks obtained in the annual and mid-sessional examination.

(ii) Only ten value areas have been taken in this study.

(iii) The study has been conducted on students of higher secondary stage (*i.e.* final year) only.

(iv) The sample for the study was drawn only from Ganjam district of Orissa.

(v) The present study was restricted to the high achievers and low achievers. Middle students have not been considered in the study.

(vi) Exclusion of middle or average students has reduced the sample size to 486.

(vii) A Descriptive research method has been used in the present study.

(viii) The statistical technique like t-test was employed.

5
DESIGN OF THE STUDY

"Scientific problem can be resolved only on the basis of the data and a major responsibility of scientist is to set up a research design capable of providing the data necessary to the solution of his problem. While the unit of research makes it impossible to say that one aspect is more crucial than another, the collection of data is of paramount importance in the conduct of research, since obviously, no solution can be more adequate than the data on which it is based"(Mouly, 1964 P.95).

The first requisite, so to speak, germane to any research is data without which no study could be conducted. Data are like raw-materials without which production in research is not possible. For collection of data, the investigator has to set up the design, *i.e.* to plan before hand. To explain the procedure used for the study, the investigator has to describe the technique used for collecting the data for his investigation. He has to describe also the reliability and validity of the tools used the method adopted in drawing out the sample and procedure employed in tabulation and organising the data.

Keeping the above fact in view, the researcher felt it essential to explain the procedure used for this study and the technique used for collecting data of this research. Thus this chapter is confined to discuss these steps as follows:

Method of the Study,
Population and Sample,
Tools Used,
Collection of Data,
Data Treatment.

METHOD OF THE STUDY

The present study has been planned and implemented under a descriptive and cross sectional framework. It aims at investigating the value patterns of higher secondary school students in relation to their academic achievement. As such the ambit of the investigation was confined to a descriptive and analytical approach. Best (1978, P.116) states:

> ***Descriptive research describes and interprets what is. It is concerned with conditions or relationships that exist; practices that Prevail; beliefs, points of view or attitudes that are held; process that are being felt; or trends that are developing.***

Of course descriptive research goes beyond more collection of data and tabulating them. It involves meaningful analysis of the data and drawing out the relevant inferences and significant conclusions. Hence, description of the investigation is obviously combined with analysis, comparison, contrast, interpretation and evaluation.

Descriptive studies are more than just a collection of data; they involve measurement, classification, analysis, comparison and interpretation. They collect and provide three types of information: (i) of what exists with respect to variables or conditions in a situation; (ii) of what we want by identifying standards or norms with which to compare the present conditions or what experts consider to be desirable; and (iii) of how to achieve goals by exploring possible ways and means on the basis of the experience of others or the opinions of experts.

So far as the research methodology is concerned, the present study comes under the scope of "Descriptive Research"; This is a status study of descriptive nature made on the basis of data gathered through field investigation. So the method, to be more exact, followed in this investigation was said to be the "Descriptive Survey". Under "causal-comparative" one.

This study would explore the casual relationship among samples those are different on the critical variables like achievement, academic stream, residential background, and sex (independent variables) but otherwise comparable on the basis of their personal value pattern scores (dependent variable). Initially it has been speculted that achievement, faculty-differences, residential background and sex (independent variables) of the higher secondary school students may have some influence on their value pattern (dependent variable) under study. Such comparative studies have been planned to be verified through this research design.

POPULATION AND SAMPLE

A population, generally refers to any collection of specified group of human beings or of non-human entities such as objects, educational institutions, time units, geographical areas, prices of wheat or salaries drawn by individuals etc. Some statisticians call it universe. Measuring the entire population is impracticable though not entirely impossible. So one has to draw a sample from the population concerned.

Population in the present study involves the students at +2 stage (*i.e.* final year only) studying in higher secondary institutions of Ganjam district (Orissa). In the district of Ganjam, the institutions providing education at +2 level may be classified into five categories. These are:

(i) Public schools, which provide education on all India pattern and depend fully on their own resources in their working.

(ii) Central schools, which provide education on all India pattern and run by central schools organisation. These are mostly meant for military personnels or central Government employees.

(iii) Government colleges, which are run by Orissa State Government and recognised and affiliated to Council of Higher Secondary Education, Orissa, Bhubaneswar.

(iv) Private Aided colleges, which are run on the grants of the Orissa State Government and recognised and affiliated to council of Higher Secondary Education, Orissa.

(v) Private colleges, which are run by private bodies and recognised and affiliated to council of Higher Secondary Education, Orissa.

Of these five types of institutions, three types of institutions (*i.e.* public School, Central Schools and private colleges) differ in their structure, functioning and management. Hence, the two types of institutions, namely Government colleges and Private Aided Colleges, which are more or less similar in their structure, functioning and management are included in the study. Thus an attempt has been made to acquire a homogeneous population by selecting the sample from the institutions having similar structural, functional and managerial style. To state it precisely, the population in the present study consists of students at +2 stage (*i.e.* final year) from Government and Private Aided colleges of Ganjam district.

The total number of institutions belonging to each type of institution, *i.e.* Government and Private Aided were found to be 5 and 31 respectively till the date of data collection December 1999. Thus, the total number of institutions spread over 22 blocks of Ganjam district was 36.

A good sample is one which is unbiased and representative of the whole population. Proportionate stratified random sampling would have been taken for the study, but keeping in view the existing number of Private Aided institutions which were comparatively larger than rest of the institutions and number of students studying in Private Aided institutions were also very large as compared to other types of institutions, it was not possible to use proportionate stratified random sampling. In stratified sampling, the population is first divided into homogeneous or administratively convenient sub-populations or strata and from each stratum a separate sample of units is selected (Srivastava and Bhatkulikar, 1980).

The purpose of the present investigation was to study the value patterns of students across the academic streams *viz*, science, arts, commerce, the unit of analysis, thus, becomes the academic stream itself. Unless and until equal (or almost equal) number of students are made available for analysis in each stream, no appropriate comparisons in value systems among students may be made. Hence, the disproportionate stratified random sampling has been employed in the present investigation. Srivastava and Bhatkulikar (1980) and Verma (1966) have mentioned that sometimes an investigator deliberately selects samples of equal size or different sizes (but not necessarily proportional to stratum size) from the different strata. This is often done to increase the representation of very small strata in the total sample, or reduce the sample size in the case of a large but homogeneous strata.

Thus, a two stage stratified disproportionate random sampling frame was adopted. The first stage of stratification pertained to the location of institutions. All institutions in the district of Ganjam were stratified into urban and rural as per the list provided by the Deputy Secretary. CHSE, Berhampur Zone, Ganjam. (cf. Table-5.1) sampled institutions.

Table - 5.1

Strata-wise composition of the Institutions

		Urban			*Rural*			
Sl. No.	*Institution*	*Boys*	*Girls*	*Coeducation*	*Boys*	*Girls*	*Coeducation*	*Total*
1.	Government	–	1	3	–	1	–	5
2.	Private Aided	–	1	1	–	1	29	32
	Total	–	2	4	–	2	29	37

In the second stage, these institutions were stratified in terms of management, (*i.e.* government and private-Aided).

The total number of government and private Aided institutions were 37. A list indicating the number of institutions in each category was then prepared. Since the number of the government institutions was less, it was decided to include all the government institutions in the study out of 32 private-Aided institutions only 06 (*i.e.* about 20%) institutions were included in the study. These 06 institutions were randomly drawn with the help of lottery method in order to get the representative samples. It was primarily decided to take at least 900 subjects, spreaded over three academic streams (*i.e.* Science, Arts and Commerce) for final analysis of the study. Thus from each academic stream a sample of 300 students was drawn randomly. Table 5.2 illustrates the total number of students spreaded over in terms of location, academic streams and sex.

Table - 5.2
Distribution of Sample Students into Different Categories

Sl. No.	*Name of the Institutions*	*Science*		*Arts*		*Commerce*	
	A-Urban	M	F	M	F	M	F
1.	Khallikota(A) College, Berhampur	55	05	20	05	60	10
2.	B.A. College, Berhampur	NP	NP	20	10	25	05
3.	Govt. Womens' College, Berhampur	–	30		20		NP
4.	M.M. Mahila Mahavidyalay, Berhampur	–	20		20		15
5.	City College, Berhampur	40	5	20	05	40	5
6.	Govt. Science College, Chatrapur	45	–	20	10	40	10
	Total	140	60	80	70	165	45

Sl. No.	Name of the Institutions	Science		Arts		Commerce	
	B-Rural	M	F	M	F	M	F
1.	Aska Science College, Aska	15	05	10	10	10	05
2.	K.S.U.B. College, Bhanjanagar	15	05	10	10	10	05
3.	Science College, Hinjilikatu	10	05	20	05	10	05
4.	R.C.M. College, Khallikote	10	05	20	10	10	05
5.	Ganjam College, Ganjam	10	05	20	10	10	05
6.	Khemundi College, Digapahandi	10	05	20	05	10	05
	Total	70	30	100	50	60	30

M = Male, F = Female
N.P. = No Provision.

A look at Table 5.2 shows that the number of institutions selected, the number of students from each academic stream, the number of rural and urban students and the number of male and female students forming part of the sample of the study are broadly representative. Thus, in all there are 560 urban students (*i.e.* 200 from Science stream, 150 from Arts stream and 210 from Commerce stream), 340 rural students (*i.e.* 100 from Science stream, 150 from Arts stream and 90 from Commerce stream), 615 male students (*i.e.* 210 from Science stream, 180 from Arts stream and 225 from Commerce stream) and 285 female students (*i.e.* 90 from Science stream, 120 from Arts stream and 75 from Commerce stream) which may be considered adequate for determining the representativeness of sample of students of the study.

TOOLS USED

While making a furniture a carpenter uses different tools. Selection of appropriate tools to be used and manner of using such tools decide the quality of the furniture he makes. Like that of a carpenter, a researcher has to select and use appropriate tools in collecting data for a project. Hence, in any investigation, suitable tools are to be chosen for use to elicit information or other such measures.

Values—The Construct and Its Measurement

In chapter-I the concept of value has been approached in detail. However, value is a conception and distinctive of an individual or of a group, of the desirable which influences the selection from the available modes, means and ends of an action. Although no social psychologists concur in their definitions of value, most of them believe that value is a concept of the desirable ends, goals, ideals, or modes of action which make human behaviour selective.

Since Thurstone (1959) averred that values could be measured by means of psychometric methods with the help of a suitable non-physical metric several attempts have been made to measure values. The efforts of Allport - Verma (1931), Precker (1952), Gordon (1956), Morris (1957), Rosenberg (1957), Dennis (1961) and Super are noteworthy.

In India most of the researchers have adapted Allport-Verma-Lindzey 'The study values' either in English or the regional languages notable are Ahluwalia (1981), Ojha (1984), Verma (1986), being other tests on values are developed by Updhyaya (1978), Agarwal (1979), Chauhan and Arora (1981), Katiyar (1982), Bansal (1986), Agarwal (1986).

Personal values questionnaire (PVQ) constructed and standardised by Sherry and Verma (1978) was employed for the present investigation (cf. Appendix-A).

Rationale Behind Using the PVQ

The personal values questionnaire (PVQ) was preferred to other available tools to measure values because of the following reasons:

(i) The PVQ provides scope for measurement of value in ten areas namely religious, social, democratic, aesthetic, economic, knowledge, hedonistic, power, family prestige and health which cover almost all value areas.

(ii) The questionnaire contains equal items in each area of value which is very appropriate for measuring value pattern.

(iii) It is comparatively easy for administration and scoring. The interpretation of raw scores is not also difficult and much technical.

(iv) Due to its easy access, a large number of Indian scholars (Mishra, 1991; Das, 1993; Nayak, 1994; Padhan, 1994; Verma *et al.*, 1995 and Srichandan, 1998) have employed it.

Characteristics of the PVQ

The main characteristics of the PVQ are as follows:

Sr. No.	*Value Areas*
A	Religious
B	Social
C	Democratic
D	Aesthetic
E	Economic
F	Knowledge
G	Hedonistic
H	Power
I	Family prestige
J	Health

The details of these are given below.

Religious Value (A)

This value is defined in terms of faith in God, attempt to understand him, fear of divine worth and acting according to the ethical codes prescribed in the religious books. The outward acts of behaviour expressive of this value are going on Pilgrimage, living a simple life, having faith in the religious leaders, worshipping God and speaking the truth.

Social Value (B)

This value is defined in terms of charity, kindness, love and sympathy for the people, efforts to serve God through the service of mankind, sacrificing personal comforts and gains to relieve the needy and the affected of their misery.

Democratic Values (C)

This value is characterised by respect for individuality, absence of discrimination among persons on the bases of sex, language, religion, caste, colour, race and family status, ensuring equal social, political and religious rights to all, impartiality and social justice and respect for the democratic institutions.

Aesthetic Value (D)

Aesthetic value is characterised by appreciation of beauty, form proportion and harmony, love for the fine arts, drawing-painting, music, dance, sculpture, poetry, and architecture, love for literature, love for decoration of the home and the surroundings, neatness and system in the arrangements of the things.

Economic Values (E)

This value stands for desire for money and material gains. A man with high economic value is guided by consideration of money and material gain in the choice of his job. His attitude towards the rich persons and the industrialists is favourable and he considers them helpful for the progress of the country.

Knowledge Value (F)

This value stands for love of knowledge of theoretical principles of any activity, and love of discovery of truth. A man with knowledge value considers a knowledge of theoretical principles underlying a work essential for success in it. He values hardwork in studies, only if it helps to develop ability to find out new facts and relationships, and aspires to be known as the seeker of knowledge. For him knowledge is virtue.

Hedonistic Value (G)

Hedonistic value as defined here, is the conception of the desirability of loving pleasure and avoiding pain. For a hedonist the present is more important than the future. A man with hedonist value indulges in pleasure of senses and avoids pains.

Power Value (H)

Here the power value is defined as the conception of desirability of ruling over others and also of leading others. The characteristics of a person of high power value are that he prefers a job where he gets opportunity to exercise authority over others, that he prefers to rule in a small place rather than serve in a big place, that the fear of law of the country rather than the fear of God deters him from having recourse to unproved means for making money and that he is deeply status-conscious and can even tell a lie for maintaining the prestige of his position.

Family Prestige Value (I)

As defined here, the family prestige value is the conception of the desirability of such items of behaviour, roles, functions and relationships as would become one's family status. It implies respect for roles which are traditionally characteristic of different castes of the Indian Society. It also implies the maintenance of the purity of family blood by avoiding inter-caste marriage. It is respect for the conservative outlook as enshrined in the traditional institution of family.

Health Value (J)

Health value is the consideration for keeping the body in a fit state for carrying out one's normal duties and functions. It also implies the consideration for self-preservation. A man with high health value really feels if through some act of negligence he impairs his health, he considers good physical health essential for the development and use of his abilities.

Reliability

Reliability of a tool is generally defined as the ratio of true variance to obtained variance of the scores (Guilford). The arrow variance component of the scores generated by a perfectly reliable tool is zero and there is no error of measurement. Hence reliability is one of the most important characteristics of a tool which denotes how accurately the tool measures whatever it measures.

Two indices of reliability of the PVQ were found out. Firstly, its reliability was determined by Hoyt's methods using analysis of variance which method is as efficient as Kuder Richardson's but less Cumbersome. Secondly, two test-retest reliabilities were determined one after an interval of "Month and the other of 2 months. Thus three sets of reliability's coefficients for the PVQ are available at present and they are presented in table-5.3".

Table - 5.3
Indices of Reliability of PVQ

		Test retest reliabilities			
Sl. No.	Values	Time gap 1 months N = 48	Time gap 3 months N = 25	Analysis Variance reliabilities N = 50	standard error or measure-ment
1.	Religious value	.52	.82	.64	1.6
2.	Social value	.45	.66	.47	1.9
3.	Democratic value	.62	.57	.48	2.4
4.	Aesthetic value	.47	.65	.56	1.8
5.	Economic value	.67	.70	.70	2.0
6.	Knowledge value	.59	.63	.50	2.2
7.	Hedonistic value	.61	.54	.63	2.0
8.	Power value	.55	.53	.60	2.1
9.	Family value	.57	.85	.67	1.6
10.	Health value	.53	4.6	.52	2.2

Evaluation of the Reliability Coefficient

It may be ovserved that the reliability coefficients obtained after a time gap of a 3 months are fairly high. The well conceptualised religious and family prestige values have reliability coefficients of .82 and .85 respectively. The lowest reliability is for the power value (.53). The reliability coefficient for other scales are in the neighbourhood of .60. Now higher reliability coefficients increase the precision of measurement by reducing its standard error. But the measurement in the field of non-intellective personality variables can not be as precise as that in the field of intelligence or achievement. Guilford (1954) says that the tools should be chosen even though their reliability may be of order of only .50 Judged from this consideration the reliability of PVQ seems to be good.

Analysis of variance method of determining reliability yielded reliability coefficients ranging from 0.47 for social value to 0.70 for the economic value. These indices of reliability of the different scales of values of PVQ are also satisfactory. In evaluating the reliability coefficients the facts that they depend on the heterogeneity of the sample and that high internal consistency is neither possible nor desirable when the variables measured from a battery to predict some criterion behaviour should be born in mind. Therefore standard error of measurement or standard error or score was calculated because this statistic compensated for the effect of variability of the variable in the sample. The last column gives the measure of this statistic for the ten values. It can be seen that the standard error of score for all the values becomes 2 on being rounded. The error of 2 score units may be considered small when the scores can vary from 0 to 24.

It is, therefore, concluded that the PVQ is a reliable tool to measure complex variables such as values.

Interpretation of Raw Score

The raw scores can be used to denote the hierarchy of the ten value in the personality of an individual after making the corrections given in Table-5.4 below. The corrections are necessary because the means for the values are not equal for a large number of persons. This difference may be attributed to unequal attractiveness of the items of different values.

Table - 5.4

Correction Figures for the Raw Scores of an Individual

Values	A	B	C	D	E	F	G	H	I	J
Correction figures	0	–4	–3	0	+3	–2	+3	+4	0	–1

The plus corrections are to be added to the raw scores of an individual and the minus corrections are to be subtracted. For example if the raw score of A on social value is 19 then his corrected score is

19–4 = 15. Similarly if the raw score of A on the power value is 8 his corrected score is 8+4=12. But the corrected score should be rarely used because the corrections are only approximate. The uses of the tool are advised to use the standard derived scores.

Derived Scores and Norms

T-scores[1] sten-scores[2] and percentile ranks for the following groups of individuals have been determined.

i. Teachers of the secondary schools.
(mixed group) (N = 674)
(a) Men teachers (N=428)
(b) Women teachers (N=246)
ii. Students of classes XI and XII N= 1725.
(a) Literary group boys (N=290)
(b) Literary group girls (N=551)
(c) Scientific group (N=631)
(d) Commerce group (N=253)
(e) Boys (N=1153)
(f) Girls (N=572)

The norms in terms of the T-scores and sten-scores can be read directly from the conversion tables given in the manual.

Interpretation of Derived Score

In order to interpret the derived scores it is essential to fix up the score-bounds for the qualitative categories. There is no universally accepted mode of conversion of the quantitative data into qualitative ones. Here an arbitrary scheme of conversion is given but it may be considered as satisfactory for most purposes.

Table - 5.5
Interpretation of Derived Score

T-scores	Sten-scores	Percentile rank	Interpretation
65 and above	9 and 10	93 and above	Very high
55-64	7 and 8	71-92	High
46-54	5 and 6	30-70	Average
35-45	3 and 4	8-29	Low
34 and above	2 and 1	7 and below	Very low

1. T-scores are standard normalised scores with a mean of 50 and S.D of 10.
2. Sten scores are standard normalised score with a mean of 5.5 and S.D of 2.

Validity of PVQ

Validity of a tool is generally defined as its capacity to measure what it purports to measure. The PVQ is designed to measure the personal values. Hence the evidence of validity of PVQ lies in the fact that an individual score on a value *e.g.* religious value, as found by means of it is truly the index of his conception of desirability of religious motivation in making choices from among the available alternative in relevant situations.

It may be stated that the evidences of validity of a tool accumulate in the course of its usage in different studies several concurrent evidences of validity of a tool are necessary to justify the claim for it. As yet only the following empirical evidences of the validity of PVQ have accumulated.

Criterion-Oriented Validity

Below are given a few criteria-oriented evidences of the validity of the ten value scale—

Religious Value

In this study it is found that the teachers who reside in Dayalbagh[1] have higher religious value than the teachers who reside in the city of Agra (P<.05). Similar result is found for the student community also (P<.05). These results are supported by other studies (Tripathi, 1966, Mathur, 1971) as well. Hence it seems resonable to say that religious scale of PVQ measures this value validity.

Social Value

The validity of the scale of PVQ is judged by comparing the value-hierarchy of B.Ed., Law, Engineering and Medical students as found by Mathur (1971), Pal (1969), Khare (1968). For the comparison only the six values of PVQ are considered.

Table - 5.6
Intra Group Rank Order of Social Value of Professional Group as Found by Different Investigators

Professional Groups	Mathur (PVQ)	Rank order as found by Pal	Khare
		Study of values	Study of values
Teaching	6	5	5
Law	3	4	4
Medicine	3	2	2
Engineering	6	4	5

The table shows that the rank order of the social value of the students of education and engineering is low in all the three investigations and that of medical students is comparatively high. The rank order of this value of low-group is somewhere in the middle of the scale in all the three studies.

It means that the social value scale of PVQ gives results comparable to those of other similar studies. It may be taken as an empirical evidence of the validity of this scale of the PVQ.

Democratic Value

In the PVQ democratic value has been defined in terms of equality for all worth of the individual and removal of discriminations on the basis of sex, caste, religious, class etc. It is therefore, expected that under-privileged sections of the society who have been discriminated against in the past, and who are struggling hard for equality in one respect or the other score higher on this value than persons who are privileged. It is found that women teachers have scored significantly higher than the men teachers (P<.5) on this value. Also the students belonging to lower strata of the society, have shown greater respect for democratic value than the students of higher strata. On the basis of the above discussion, it seems plausible that PVQ measures democratic value truely.

Aesthetic Value

From the study of the standardisation sample, the girl of the literary group (N-551) are found to have a significantly higher (p<.100) mean on aesthetic value than the boys of the same group. The difference between the aesthetic value of the total groups of girls (N=572) and boys (N=1153) is also found significant (P<.01). Girls have an edge over the boys in this value. Similarly women teachers (N=246) are found to be significantly higher than the men teachers (N=421) in respect of this value (P<0.1). These findings are supported by the norms on the aesthetic value of men and women given by Ray Chaudhary (1958), who has also found out that women are higher than men in their aesthetic value. Thus it seems justified to say that PVQ measures aesthetic value validity.

Economic Value

From the study of the value of the standardisation sample, it is observed that students of commerce group (N=253) most of whom belong to business communities are higher in their economic value than the student of scientific group (N=631)(P<.01). This is an evidence of the fact that economic scale of the PVQ measures this value validity.

Knowledge Value

Validity of the knowledge value scale of the PVQ is established by the fact that students of scientific grap (N=631) are found higher in knowledge value than students of literary (N=290) and commerce groups (N=253), (P<.01). Using PVQ as tool engineering students were found to be higher in their knowledge value than the students of law and education. Using Allport-Verma-Lindzey "Study of Value". Khare (1968), also found that engineers were significantly higher than professors and advocates in their theoretical (knowledge) value. It means that the knowledge value scale of PVQ differentiates among the professional groups in the expected manner.

The aforesaid empirical findings suggest that the knowledge value scale of the PVQ is valid.

Hedonistic Value

The only evidence of the validity of this value that has as yet been obtained is that in a school a group of 6 teachers who were habitual drinkers, were found to be high on this value. We feel that more convincing evidences of the validity of this value are needed.

Power Value

In a patriarchal society, boys are expected to have higher power value than girls because they yet opportunities for developing this value. Hence the validity of the power value scale is clear from the findings of the present study where boys of literary group (N=290) have shown significantly higher (P<.01) power value than the girls of the same group (N=551). In another study using PVQ as a tool for measuring values of professional students Mathur (1971) found that students of Engineering held power value in significantly less esteem than the students of education (B.Ed classes) (P<.05). This finding of here is corroborated by the finding of Pal (1969) who used Ray Chaudhary's adaptation of Allport *et al.* "Study of values" These evidences support the validity of this scale of value.

Family Prestige Value

At regards the validity of family prestige value it is supported by the fact that teachers of the school situated in the city. Now it may be stated that Dayalbagh is a casteless society where the marriages are mostly inter-caste. Here the worth of an individual is measured in terms of his personal accomplishments and not in terms of the accidents of his birth in a high and/or rich family. So it is natural that the residents of Dayalbagh attach very low importance to the family prestige value. Family prestige is belived to be high among individual coming from conservative families which abound in rural areas Mathur on PVQ (1971) found that student-teachers with rural orientation were very high in their family prestige value. Women teachers are found to be lower in family prestige value than men teachers (P<.05) in this study. The findings that women teachers are low in family prestige value seems to be plausible because women choosing a career is itself a break from traditionalism which is implied in the family prestige value. Hence the family prestige value scale of the PVQ seems to be valid.

Health Value

Validity of the health value is supported by the fact that men teachers (N=428) have significantly higher health value than the women teachers (N=246; P<.01). The same is true of boys (N=1153) and girls (N=572). It may be recalled here that the health value in the PVQ means the valuing of health making practices like morning walk, exercise, playing etc. among other things. Now it is generally observed that woman do not value wealth to the extent that they prefer these practices to a activities signifying other values. Hence it is quite natural that women scores significantly lower than men on this value. And health value scale of the PVQ which reveals this sex difference is, therefore, valid.

Above evidences of different scale of values incorporated in PVQ are only tentative and still stranger evidences are needed to confirm their validity.

Validity Via Correlation

Although validity coefficients are liable to be deceptive and should not be accepted yet they prove to be useful indices of validity if the heterogeneity of sample and other factors are kept in view in obtaining them. The validity of PVQ was obtained by finding out the hierarchy of values of sample of 20 psychology students of B.A. part II in two ways. Firstly they were administered PVQ and the hierarchy of their ten values was determined. Then they were asked to rank the ten values. The ten values were functionally defined in terms of the contents of the PVQ. The two hierarchies were correlated and the rank order coefficient of correction of .64 was found. This correlation is significant at 0.5 level (df=8). Thus it may be said that the PVQ is a fairly valid tool to determine the hierarchy of values of a group. It may be remarked here that the foregoing evidence of the validity of PVQ are fairly strong.

Administration of the PVQ

PVQ may be administered individually as well as in a group. It should be filled out under the standard instructions. First the respondents should fill up the personal data blank printed on the front page. But they should be clearly instructed not to fill up the page which is meant for the investigator. When all the respondents have filled up the blank they should be asked to turn over the page. The investigator should read out the instructions printed on page I of the PVQ loudly and clearly. The respondents should follow him carefully. He should explain the mode of filling out the PVQ very carefully, He should explain the mode filling out the PVQ very carefully, preferably with the help of a black board if one is available there. When he is sure that they have understood the mode of recording their responses, he should permit them to turn over the page, and ask them to record their responses. He should invigilate the respondent while they are filling up the PVQ lest they should consult one another.

Collection of PVQ

There is no time limit for filling out the questionnaire. Therefore a respondent should be permitted to return it when he has completed it. Time permitting the investigator should summarily see if all the questions have been answered by the respondent. The administration of the PVQ was ended with a thank by the investigator.

The respondents asked two questions when they were requested to fill out the PVQ. Firstly, they asked the utility of filling it out. Secondly, they were keen to know the result. in reply to the first question they were told that the purpose of this tool was to find out the value system of the present day people of their class (students or teachers or any other group of people as the case may be.) Their responses would be the basis of the inferences to be drawn. In reply to the second question they were told that the result will be reported in the form of a research finding and any one of them interested in the findings may approach him after some time in the first week of the January 1999.

Scoring of the PVQ

The responses are to be scored as follows:

1. 2 for a check mark (✓) showing the most preferred value under the stem.
2. 0 for a cross (×) showing the least preferred value under the stem.
3. 1 for the (✓) or unmarked item showing the intermediate preference for the value.

Sometimes the respondents leave some questions unanswered. If the number of such questions is 4 or less, each item of the unanswered question should be scored as 1. If their number is more than 4 the questionnaire should be rejected.

In all the cases the scores should be recorded beside the corresponding bracket and the total for each value (A to J) should be written in the cage given at the foot of the page. The correctness of scoring and recording of the totals for all the values is checked by summing the total for all of them on each page separately. If the grand total is 24 the. scoring may be correct provided that compensating errors have not been committed.

Finally the entries in the cage at the foot of each page should be brought to the bigger cage on the front page of the PVQ. The total of each column should be noted down in the bottom row. These totals denote the scores of the respondents on the corresponding value given at the top or column. In this questionnaire.

(i) A stands for the religious value.
(ii) B stands for the social value.
(iii) C stands for the democratic value.

(iv) D stands for the aesthetic value.
(v) E stands for the economic value.
(vi) F stands for the knowledge value.
(vii) G stands for the hedonistic value.
(viii) H stands for the power value.
(ix) I stands for the family prestige value.
(x) J stands for the health value.

Academic Achievement—The Construct and its Measurement

In the modern society, the parents, teachers and educators are worried about the better grade of the students on scholastic achievement. The children are sent to school to achieve better grade through formal education. To achieve the status in the society, the importance of academic attainment can not be neglected.

It is the duties of the school to foster the achievement in scholastic areas. The academic achievement can be estimated through testing so in the field of education attempts are made to assess the academic achievement in the form of scores.

In the absence of standardised tests in various subjects—physics, chemistry, biology, mathematics, history, geography, economics, commerce, home science, psychology etc.—the data regarding achievement in these academic subjects were collected through the average of the marks in the annual examination of classes IX and X and the half-yearly examination of class XI. Many investigators have used the school marks for determining the academic achievement Sharma (1968) found the reliability and validity of the school marks as a satisfactory measure for use in research studies Passi (1971) used the school achievement scores in school subjects taking the percentage of aggregate marks obtained in the middle standard examination.

On these grounds it was decided not to mako usc of any specific achievement test in the present study but to use the average of the marks in the annual examination of class XI and the half-yearly examination of class XII.

COLLECTION OF DATA

The subjects of this study were selected from the prescribed population. Names of the institutions, number of subjects from different streams etc. from which the samples were drawn have already been given in tables 5.1 and 5.2. The principal of these institutions were approached one by one and the objectives of this study were explained. Almost all the principals provided the facilities for collection of data.

The selected students were administered the personal values questionnaire (PVQ) in the classes of their respective institutions.

Necessary rapport was established through personal contacts. The purpose of the study was explained to them. The subjects were requested to answer the questions sincerely and frankly. They were assured that the responses would be kept strictly confidential. They were further requested to write their percentage of marks in the last three consequitive examinations at the top of the first page of the answer sheet. The marks recorded by them were verified from the result sheets of the college.

The completed response sheet of each student was scored according to the instructions given for the scoring procedure. The raw scores were converted or the T-scores for their use.

DATA TREATMENT

The main purpose of this study was to compare the values of students belonging to different academic streams. The data obtained on values (cf Appendix-B) for each stream (N=300) were tabulated separately into frequency distributions. Mean scores and SDs of each group on values were calculated. Profiles for different groups were prepared on the basis of mean scores and plotted in figures to give a comparative picture.

Frequency distributions for all the groups were approximately normal. Hence the comparison between different groups was made on the basis of the t-test with 0.05 and 0.01 levels of confidence considered significant.

In order to compare the high achievers and low achievers on their personal values p-75 and p-25 were calculated respectively for identifying the high achievers and low achievers.

As the nature of the study was to identify and compare personal values of high and low achievers, achievement scores for all the students (*i.e.* stream-wise) were arranged in descending order. To have two sharp groups of high achievers and low achievers demonstrating their respective peculiarities, 27% criteria (Kelly's dichotomy) was used. Thus, 81 students from each stream and altogether 243 high achievers and 81 students from each stream and in all 243 low achievers were selected.

6

ANALYSIS AND INTERPRETATION OF DATA

The present study, as stated earlier, aims at exploring the value profiles of higher secondary students belonging to different academic streams (*i.e.* science, arts and commerce) and thereby comparing them and comparing value patterns of high and low achievers across their academic streams. A comparison between the value patterns of the students having rural and urban background, and between the male and female students have also been made to study as to whether there was any significant difference between the two groups respectively on each of the value areas. The design and methodology employed for conducting the study have been discussed in the preceding chapter. In order to maintain the logical sequence and ease in presentation of results and formulation of findings, the whole analysis has been divided into three main parts. The first part deals with distribution of scores on values and academic achievement of the total sample to examine in respect of their nature and departure from normalcy. The second part deals with exploration of students value profiles which includes academic stream, residential background, sex and achievement level as the main points of presentation. The third part comprises comparison of different groups (*i.e.* streamwise, residential background-wise, sex-wise and achievement level-wise) on value patterns In the following pages, is available a systematic and comprehensive analysis of data and their interpretation as referred to here.

STUDY OF THE DISTRIBUTION OF VALUES AND ACADEMIC ACHIEVEMENT SCORES

The main thrust of the investigation was to study the value of higher secondary students across their academic streams, namely science, arts and commerce in relation to the achievement. For the purpose a total sample of 900 students (*i.e.* 300 from each stream) were administered the personal value questionnaire developed by Sherry and Verma (1978). The distributions of scores on values and academic achievement were examined in respect of their nature and departure from normalcy. The assumption of normality is that the dependent variable in the population from which the samples have been drawn should be normally distributed. To be sure of the satisfaction of this assumption indices of Skewness and Kurtosis were computed following the percentile method (Garrett, 1975). The values of Skewness, Kurtosis for different ten values of science, arts and commerce students together with the academic achievement have been given in Table 6.1.

Table - 6.1
Values of Skewness and Kurtosis of Values and Academic Achievement

Sr. No.	Variable	Science sk	Science ku	Arts sk	Arts ku	Commerce sk	Commerce ku
1	Religious (A)	-2.33	0.23	-0.55	0.34	0.43	0.26
2.	Social (B)	-2.81	0.24	0.41	0.29	0.46	0.31
3.	Democratic (C)	-1.86	0.31	-3.96	0.31	-.71	0.24
4.	Aesthetic (D)	-2.10	0.23	-2.45	0.29	-.85	0.29
5.	Economic (E)	0.17	0.26	-4.30	0.23	-.93	0.23
6.	Knowledge (F)	-2.79	0.25	-0.52	0.19	-.73	0.27
7.	Hedonistic (G)	-0.78	0.24	-2.09	0.21	-2.49	0.35
8.	Power (H)	-3.12	0.27	-0.31	0.33	-3.19	0.29
9.	Family Prestige (I)	-1.63	0.26	-1.14	0.31	-1.11	0.28
10.	Health (J)	-2.88	0.22	-1.28	0.28	-.30	0.33
11.	B-Academic Achievement (Total)	sk -1.88	ku 0.28				

The values of Skewness and Kurtosis in Table 6.1 for all the dependent variables, except a few ones, indicated near normality. Boneau (1960) says:

That in a large number of research situations, the probability statements resulting from the use of 't' and 'F' tests, even when these two assumptions of homogeneity and normality are violated will be highly accurate.

In the light of the remarks given above it was decided to use 't' test for all the variables.

VALUES OF STUDENTS—THE PROFILE ANALYSIS

In pursuance of the objective 1 of the study to determine the value profiles of the higher secondary students across their academic stream, residential background, sex and achievement level, the scores on the personal value Questionnaire (PVQ) were subjected to the computation of mean and S.D. In addition the ranks assigned to each value type by the students belonging to different academic streams, residential background, sex and achievement level were ordered to see whether there is any unique value pattern existing among those groups or there is deviation in the line. These results are shown in Table 6.2 through Table 6.9.

Study of Value Profiles Across the Academic Streams

In the present study the students from three academic streams, namely science, arts and commerce have been considered and their personal values, as reflected through the Sherry and Verma (1978) PVQ, were computed in terms of mean and S.D. The relevant results are presented in Table 6.2 and 6.3.

On a general observation of Tables 6.2 and 6.3, it seems that students belonging to three different academic streams (*i.e.* Science, Arts and Commerce) in the study have their own unique value profiles, where similarity regarding the preference of certain values are evident. From Table 6.2 where the categorisation was mainly based on academic stream, it has been found that the value profile encompassed the highest preference for power values among arts and commerce students along with their matched least preference for social values with slight difference in the magnitudes of mean and SD values of these preferences in two different categories of students' samples. Yet their resemblances in ranking of these two values were maintained properly. On the other hand, the Science students ranked highest to hedonistic values and lowest to social values Fig. 1 gives a comparative picture of the value profiles of the science, arts and commerce students under consideration. Further more, Table 6.3 clearly revealed the similarity in ranks of health values as last but one (*i.e.* 9th rank) religious values (*i.e.* 6th rank), Family Prestige values (*i.e.* 5th rank), aesthetic values (*i.e.* 4th rank) and in the three groups of students economic values (*i.e.* 3rd rank). There were diviations in value profiles in respect to the positions of hedonistic, power, democratic and knowledge values. In this context it has been noted that hedonistic value occupied the first preference for the science students, whereas

Table - 6.2
Mean and S.D. of Value Scores Alongwith the Value Ranks for Three Groups of Students

Values	Science			Arts			Commerce		
	M	SD	Rank	M	SD	Rank	M	SD	Rank
Religious (A)	45.08	9.0	6	44.61	8.30	6	43.74	8.24	6
Social (B)	22.53	10.39	10	24.14	9.04	10	21.51	9.45	10
Democratic (C)	43.43	8.29	7	38.15	7.47	8	37.69	8.54	8
Aesthetic (D)	55.06	9.47	4	53.56	9.86	4	55.49	10.06	4
Economic (E)	56.32	11.71	3	54.55	11.80	3	59.41	10.49	3
Knowledge (F)	41.77	8.69	8	40.48	8.06	7	40.16	7.69	7
Hedonistic (G)	65.93	7.33	1	64.51	7.59	2	65.52	7.96	2
Power (H)	63.75	9.16	2	66.73	8.15	1	68.17	7.88	1
Family Prestige (I)	51.11	7.9	5	51.41	8.78	5	49.80	8.43	5
Health (J)	36.15	7.27	9	36.34	6.47	9	35.87	7.61	9

Table - 6.3
Successive Positions of Each Value in Three Groups of Students

Positions of value	1	2	3	4	5	6	7	8	9	10
Science	HC	P	E	A	FP	R	D	K	Hh	S
Arts	P	HC	E	A	FP	R	K	D	Hh	S
Commerce	P	HC	E	A	FP	R	K	D	Hh	S

Table - 6.4
Mean and S.D. of Value Scores Alongwith the Value Ranks of Rural and Urban Students

	Rural			Urban		
Values	M	SD	Rank	M	SD	Rank
Religious (A)	49.90	9.20	7	59.41	12.10	6
Social (B)	52.52	9.87	2	56.92	10.81	8
Democratic (C)	54.83	11.36	1	62.08	10.78	1
Aesthetic (D)	52.32	10.74	3	60.60	10.80	3
Economic (E)	51.11	10.25	5	54.56	9.68	9
Knowledge (F)	50.15	10.78	6	60.22	9.31	4
Hedonistic (G)	51.22	9.59	4	59.92	8.45	5
Power (H)	46.62	8.90	9	60.90	9.14	2
Family Prestige (I)	49.66	10.35	8	58.55	10.19	7
Health (J)	45.87	9.89	10	52.04	9.14	10

Table - 6.5
Successive Positions of Each Value in Two Different Groups of Students

Positions of value	1	2	3	4	5	6	7	8	9	10
Rural	D	S	A	Hc	E	K	R	FP	P	Hh
Urban	D	P	A	K	Hc	R	FP	S	E	Hh

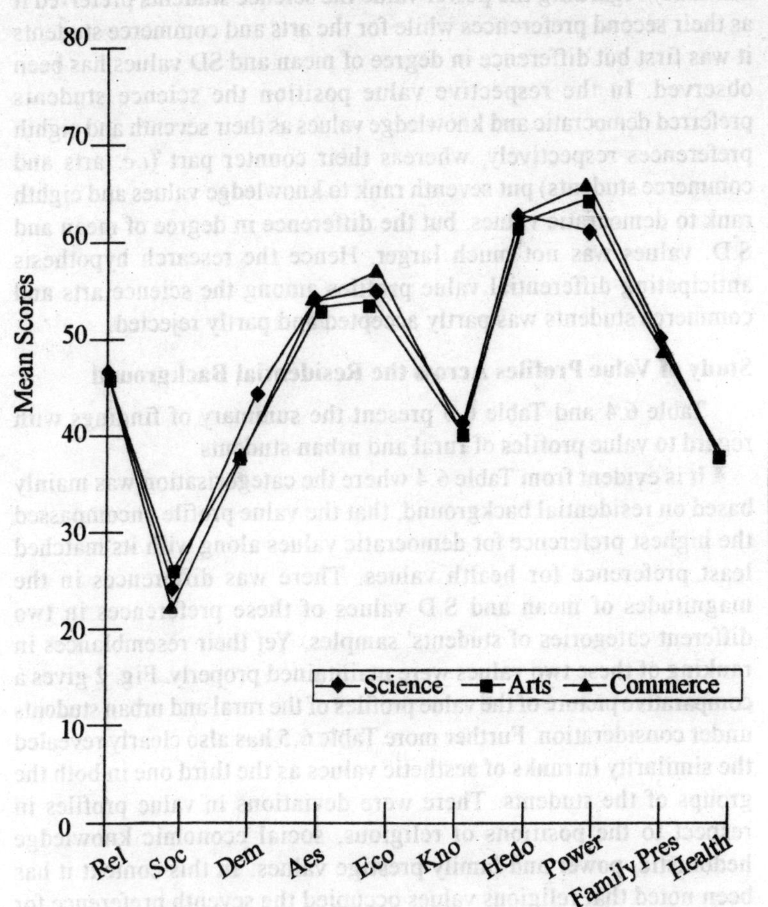

FIG. 1 : VALUE PROFILES OF SCIENCE, ARTS AND COMMERCE STUDENTS

it had second position in the value profiles of arts and commerce students though the mean and SD values did not differ much in degree. Similarly regarding the power value the science students preferred it as their second preferences while for the arts and commerce students it was first but difference in degree of mean and SD values has been observed. In the respective value position the science students preferred democratic and knowledge values as their seventh and eighth preferences respectively, whereas their counter part (*i.e.* arts and commerce students) put seventh rank to knowledge values and eighth rank to democratic values, but the difference in degree of mean and S.D. values was not much larger. Hence the research hypothesis anticipating differential value profiles among the science arts and commerce students was partly accepted and partly rejected.

Study of Value Profiles Across the Residential Background

Table 6.4 and Table 6.5 present the summary of findings with regard to value profiles of rural and urban students.

It is evident from Table 6.4 where the categorisation was mainly based on residential background, that the value profile encompassed the highest preference for democratic values along with its matched least preference for health values. There was differences in the magnitudes of mean and S.D values of these preferences in two different categories of students' samples. Yet their resemblances in ranking of these two values were maintained properly. Fig. 2 gives a comparative picture of the value profiles of the rural and urban students under consideration. Further more Table 6.5 has also clearly revealed the similarity in ranks of aesthetic values as the third one in both the groups of the students. There were deviations in value profiles in respect to the positions of religious, social economic knowledge hedonistic, power and family prestige values. In this context it has been noted that religious values occupied the seventh preference for the rural students, whereas it had sixth position in the value profiles of the urban students, with the larger difference in degree of mean and S.D. values. Similarly regarding the social values the groups had been found to differ much in their rankings with the difference in degree of mean and S.D. values. In the respective value position the rural students preferred economic values as their fifth preferences, whereas their counterpart put ninth rank to it. But there was slight differences in the magnitudes of mean and S.D. values of these preferences in two different categories of students' samples. There

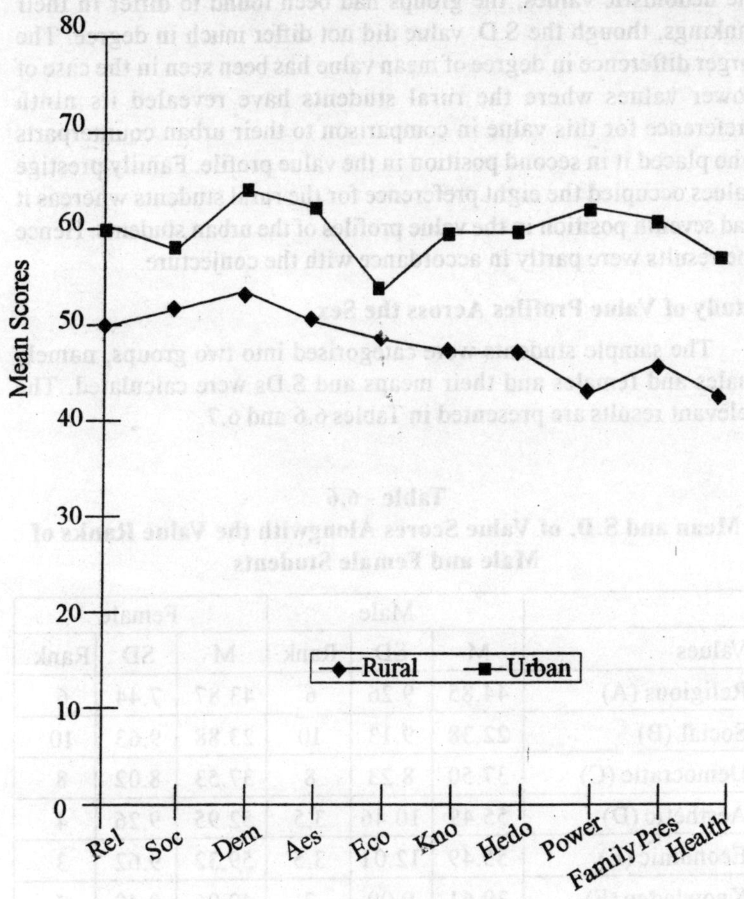

FIG. 2 : VALUES PROFILES OF RURAL AND URBAN STUDENTS

was large difference in degree of mean, but slight difference in S.D. values in the case of knowledge values where the rural students have revealed its sixth preference for this value in comparison to the urban students who placed it in fourth position in the value profile. Regarding the hedonistic values, the groups had been found to differ in their rankings, though the S.D. value did not differ much in degree. The larger difference in degree of mean value has been seen in the case of power values where the rural students have revealed its ninth preference for this value in comparison to their urban counterparts who placed it in second position in the value profile. Family prestige values occupied the eight preference for the rural students whereas it had seventh position in the value profiles of the urban students. Hence the results were partly in accordance with the conjecture.

Study of Value Profiles Across the Sex

The sample students were categorised into two groups, namely males and females and their means and S.Ds were calculated. The relevant results are presented in Tables 6.6 and 6.7.

Table - 6.6
Mean and S.D. of Value Scores Alongwith the Value Ranks of Male and Female Students

	Male			Female		
Values	M	SD	Rank	M	SD	Rank
Religious (A)	44.85	9.26	6	43.87	7.44	6
Social (B)	22.38	9.13	10	23.88	9.63	10
Democratic (C)	37.50	8.23	8	37.53	8.02	8
Aesthetic (D)	55.49	10.46	3.5	52.95	9.26	4
Economic (E)	55.49	12.01	3.5	59.32	9.62	3
Knowledge (F)	39.61	9.00	7	40.06	9.48	7
Hedonistic (G)	65.36	7.56	2	62.35	9.17	1
Power (H)	68.65	7.25	1	61.49	10.72	2
Family Prestige (I)	51.08	7.88	5	48.34	8.57	5
Health (J)	36.69	7.00	9	35.49	7.66	9

Table - 6.7
Successive Positions of Each Value in Two Different Groups of Students

Positions of value	1	2	3	4	5	6	7	8	9	10
Male Female	P Hc	Hc P	A E	E A	FP FP	R R	K K	D D	Hh Hh	S S

Table - 6.8
Mean and S.D. of Value Scores Alongwith the Value Ranks of High and Low Achievers

	High Achievers			Low Achievers		
Values	M	SD	Rank	M	SD	Rank
Religious (A)	45.55	9.20	6	44.10	10.9	6
Social (B)	22.62	9.72	10	26.24	9.67	10
Democratic (C)	38.34	9.80	8	37.05	7.16	8
Aesthetic (D)	54.59	9.85	4	54.30	11.15	3
Economic (E)	60.12	10.40	3	53.36	13.25	4
Knowledge (F)	39.18	9.93	7	41.09	10.81	7
Hedonistic (G)	66.14	10.36	2	62.98	8.94	2
Power (H)	66.75	9.54	1	64.19	10.98	1
Family Prestige (I)	50.18	8.57	5	49.93	8.75	5
Health (J)	35.72	7.57	9	35.18	9.48	9

Table - 6.9
Successive Positions of Each Value in Two Different Groups of Students

Positions of value	1	2	3	4	5	6	7	8	9	10
High Achievers	P	Hc	E	A	FP	R	K	D	Hh	S
Low Achievers	P	Hc	A	E	FP	R	K	D	Hh	S

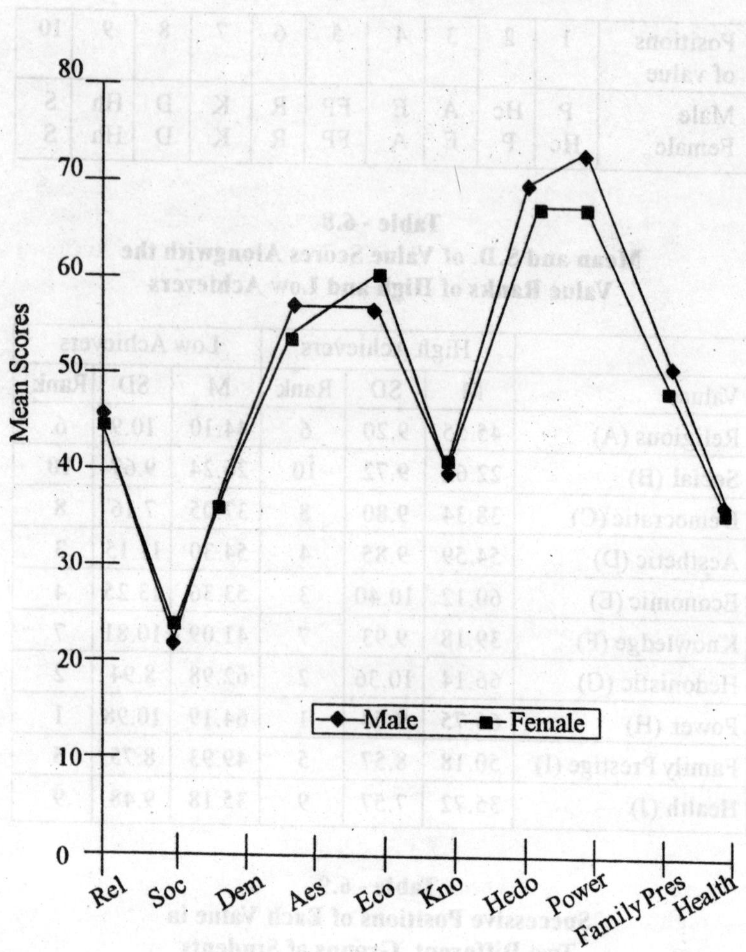

FIG. 3 : VALUE PROFILES OF MALE AND FEMALE STUDENTS

A cursory look at Table 6.6 indicates that both the groups of students in the study have their unique value profiles, where similarity regarding the preference of certain values are evident. From the table (*i.e.* Table 6.6) where the categorisation was mainly based on sex, it has been found that the value profile encompassed the highest preference for power values and hedonistic values among male and female students respectively along with its matched least preference for social values. It is most striking to note that the male and female students did not have the matched highest preference Fig. 3 gives a comparative picture of the value profile of the male and female students. Further more Table 6.7 has also revealed the similarity in ranks of health values as last but one (*i.e.* 9th rank), democratic (*i.e.* 8th rank), knowledge (*i.e.* 7th rank), religious (*i.e.* 6th rank), and family prestige (*i.e.* 5th rank). It is most striking to note that the male students preferred aesthetic and economic values equally (cf Table 6.6). On the other hand the female students preferred economic and aesthetic values as their third and fourth preferences respectively. One can note deviations in value profiles in respect to the position of hedonistic and power values. In this context it has been noted that hedonistic values occupied the second highest preference for the male students, whereas power values occupied the second highest preference for the female students. Hence the research hypothesis of differential value profiles of male and female student stood rejected in case of six values where similarity regarding the preferences were evident.

Study of Value Profiles Across the Academic Achievement

The sampled students were categorised into two groups, namely high achievers and low achievers and their means and S.Ds were calculated. The results are given in Tables 6.8 and 6.9.

From Table 6.8 where the categorisation was mainly based on achievement level it has been found that the value profile encompassed the highest preference for power values along with its matched least preference for social values. There was slight differences in the magnitudes of mean and S.D. values of these preferences in two different categories of students samples. Yet their resemblances in ranking of these two values were maintained properly. Fig 4 gives a comparative picture of the value profiles of the high and low achievers. Furthermore, Table 6.9 has also revealed the similarity in ranks of health values as last but one (*i.e.* 9th rank), democratic values (*i.e.* 8th rank), knowledge values (*i.e.* 7th rank), religious values (*i.e.* 6th rank), family prestige value (*i.e.* 5th rank), and hedonistic values (*i.e.*

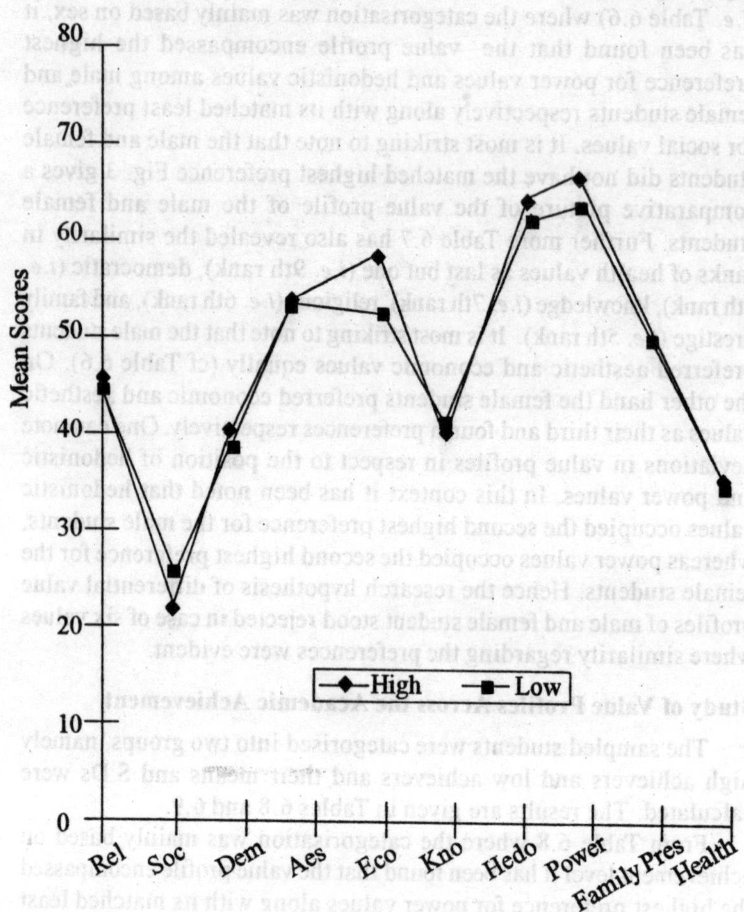

FIG. 4 : VALUE PROFILES OF HIGH AND LOW ACHIEVERS

2nd rank), in both the groups of the students. There were deviations in value profiles in respect to the positions of economic and aesthetic values. In this context it has been observed that economic values occupied the third preference for the high achievers whereas it had fourth position in the value profiles of low achievers, with the larger difference in degree of mean and S.D. values. Similarly regarding the aesthetic value the groups had been found to differ in their rankings though the mean and S.D. values did not differ much in degree. Hence the research hypothesis was accepted in case of two personal values (*i.e.* economic and aesthetic).

Table - 6.10

Significance of Difference in Mean Scores on Values of Science and Arts Students

		Science N=300		Arts N=300		
Sl.	Values	M	SD	M	SD	t-value
1.	Religious (A)	45.08	9.00	44.61	8.3	0.66
2.	Social (B)	22.53	10.39	24.14	9.04	2.02*
3.	Democratic (C)	43.43	8.29	38.15	7.47	8.19**
4.	Aesthetic (D)	55.06	9.47	53.56	9.86	1.90
5.	Economic (E)	56.32	11.71	54.55	11.8	1.84
6.	Knowledge (F)	41.77	8.69	40.48	8.06	1.88
7.	Hedonistic (G)	65.93	7.33	64.51	7.59	2.33*
8.	Power (H)	63.75	9.16	66.73	8.15	4.21**
9.	Family Prestige (I)	51.11	7.9	51.41	8.78	0.44
10.	Health (J)	36.15	7.27	36.34	6.47	0.34

* P < .05

** P < .01

COMPARISON OF VALUES OF HIGHER SECONDARY STUDENTS BELONGING TO DIFFERENT ACADEMIC STREAMS

An attempt has been made here to compare the values of higher secondary students belonging to three different academic streams, namely science, arts and commerce. It was hypothesised that value patterns of students as represented by three different academic streams (*i.e.* science, arts and commerce) of higher secondary education will be significantly different. In order to test this hypothesis comparisons were made between science and arts students, between science and commerce students, and between arts and commerce students on values as measured by PVQ (Sherry and Verma, 1978). The derived scores (*i.e.* T-scores) obtained by science, arts and commerce students on ten values namely religious, social, democratic, aesthetic, economic, knowledge, hedonistic, power, family prestige and health were tabulated separately into frequency distributions. Mean scores and S.D.s for each group on ten scales were calculated. Comparison among the groups were made on the basis of the 't'- test with 0.05 level and 0.01 level of confidence for significance. The relevant results are summarised in Table 6.10 through Table 6.12.

Table - 6.11
Significance of Difference in Mean Scores on Values of Science and Commerce Students

		Science N=300		Comm. N=300		
Sl.	Values	M	SD	M	SD	t-value
1.	Religious (A)	45.08	9.00	43.74	8.24	1.70
2.	Social (B)	22.53	10.39	21.51	9.45	1.26
3.	Democratic (C)	43.43	8.29	37.69	8.54	8.35**
4.	Aesthetic (D)	55.06	9.47	55.49	10.06	0.54
5.	Economic (E)	56.32	11.71	59.41	10.49	3.40**
6.	Knowledge (F)	41.77	8.69	40.16	7.69	2.40*
7.	Hedonistic (G)	65.93	7.33	65.52	7.96	0.66
8.	Power (H)	63.75	9.16	68.17	7.88	6.33**
9.	Family Prestige (I)	51.11	7.9	49.8	8.43	1.97*
10.	Health (J)	36.15	7.27	35.87	7.61	0.46

* P<0.05
** P<0.01

A close perusal of Table 6.10 revealed significance of difference between science and arts students on values like social (t=2.02, df 598, p<.05), democratic (t=8.19 df 598, p<.01), hedonistic (t=2.33 df 598, p<.05) and power (t=4.21, df 598, p<.01). This suggests that science and arts students differed significantly with respect to their social democratic, hedonistic and power values. On the basis of the comparison of their mean scores it can be said that science students were more democratic and hedonistic than their arts counterparts. On the other hand the arts students had higher preferences for social and power values than their science counterparts. Hence the hypothesis of significant differences in value patterns was accepted with regard to foregoing four values. However, both the science and arts students were found to be similar with regard to religious, aesthetic, economic, knowledge, family prestige and health values. Here the hypothesis anticipating significant difference in values of both the groups was rejected.

Table - 6.12
Significance of Difference in Mean Scores on Values of Arts and Commerce Students

		Arts N=300		Comm.N=300		
Sl.	Values	M	SD	M	SD	t-value
1.	Religious (A)	44.61	8.3	43.74	8.24	1.29
2.	Social (B)	24.14	9.04	21.51	9.45	3.48**
3.	Democratic (C)	38.15	7.47	37.69	8.54	0.70
4.	Aesthetic (D)	53.56	9.86	55.49	10.06	2.37*
5.	Economic (E)	54.55	11.8	59.41	10.49	5.33**
6.	Knowledge (F)	40.48	8.06	40.16	7.69	0.50
7.	Hedonistic (G)	64.51	7.59	65.52	7.96	1.59
8.	Power (H)	66.73	8.15	68.17	7.88	2.20*
9.	Family Prestige (I)	51.41	8.78	49.8	8.43	2.29*
10.	Health (J)	36.34	6.47	35.87	7.61	0.82

* P<0.05
** p<0.01

The statistical analysis (vide Table 6.11) revealed that science and commerce students differed significantly in respect to their mean scores on five values (democratic, t=8.35, p<0.01; economic, t=3.40, p<0.01; knowledge (t=2.40, p<.05; power t=6.33, p<.01 and family prestige, t= 1.97, p>0.05). It may be noted that science students yielded significantly higher values on democratic, knowledge and family prestige scales while the commerce students indicated significantly higher values on economic and power scales. Both the groups, however occupied the similar position in case of the remaining five values (*i.e.* religious, social aesthetic, hedonistic and health). Hence the research hypothesis was partly accepted in those five values where significant difference was noted and partly rejected in those five values where significant difference was not noted.

Table - 6.13
Comparison of Rural and Urban Students on Values

		Rural N=340		Urban N=560		
Sl.	Values	M	SD	M	SD	t-value
1.	Religious (A)	49.90	9.20	59.41	12.10	13.31*
2.	Social (B)	52.52	9.87	56.92	10.81	6.25**
3.	Democratic (C)	54.83	11.36	62.08	10.78	9.46**
4.	Aesthetic (D)	52.32	10.74	60.69	10.80	11.31**
5.	Economic (E)	51.11	10.25	54.56	9.68	5.00**
6.	Knowledge (F)	50.15	10.78	60.22	9.31	14.29**
7.	Hedonistic (G)	51.22	9.59	59.92	8.45	13.79**
8.	Power (H)	46.62	8.90	60.90	9.14	23.10**
9.	Family Prestige (I)	49.66	10.35	58.55	10.19	12.57**
10.	Health (J)	45.87	9.89	52.04	9.14	9.33**

* P<0.05
** P<0.01

The results as projected in Table 6.12 conclude that arts and commerce students differed significantly on five values like social (t=3.48, p<.01), aesthetic (t=2.37, p<0.05), economic (t=5.33, p<.01), power (t=2.20, p<.05) and family prestige (t=2.29, p<.05). The arts students had shown higher mean scores on social and family prestige values in comparison to their commerce counterparts, whereas on aesthetic, economic and power values, commerce students had scored significantly higher mean values than the arts students on the basis of these results, it may be said that arts students appear to have high social and family prestige values as against their commerce counterpart students and the commerce students seem to have high aesthetic, economic and power values than the arts students. On the rest of the values arts and commerce students were found to be alike. Hence the research hypothesis was partly accepted and partly rejected.

COMPARISON OF VALUES OF STUDENTS HAVING RURAL AND URBAN BACKGROUNDS

In pursuance of the objective (*i.e.* in chapter 4) of the study 'to compare the value patterns of higher secondary students having rural-urban background' significance of difference between relevant means were tested by employing 't'- test. The obtained results have been presented below in order to test the concerned hypothesis.

Table - 6.14
Comparison of Arts Rural and Science Rural Students on Values

		Arts Rural N=150		Science Rural N=100		
Sl.	Values	M	SD	M	SD	t-value
1.	Religious (A)	50.28	9.23	50.26	9.29	0.01
2.	Social (B)	52.25	10.16	60.15	10.26	5.99**
3.	Democratic (C)	49.15	11.34	63.19	12.50	8.77**
4.	Aesthetic (D)	48.29	10.62	59.16	11.92	7.37**
5.	Economic (E)	54.26	12.26	48.96	9.25	3.89**
6.	Knowledge (F)	58.15	14.61	46.19	9.23	7.93**
7.	Hedonistic (G)	55.60	11.19	55.16	10.29	0.32
8.	Power (H)	43.21	9.15	51.28	9.24	6.79**
9.	Family Prestige (I)	46.62	10.21	54.16	10.60	5.59**
10.	Health (J)	44.18	9.65	49.26	10.23	3.93**

* P<0.05
** P<0.01

This hypothesis maintains that there will be significant differences in values patterns of higher secondary students belonging to rural and urban backgrounds and among other sub groups.

The results of analysis with regard to significance of difference in means of students' personal values for rural and urban students together with various subgroups are presented in Table-6.13 through Table 6.2.

Table 6.13 presents results pertaining to the significance of difference between means of rural and urban students on values.

It may be gathered from Table 6.13 that all the t-values for groupings based on residential background (*i.e.* rural vs. urban) of students were found to be significant at .01 level of confidence. Results revealed that the students having urban background had scored significantly higher mean scores on all the ten values namely religious, social, democratic, aesthetic, economic, knowledge, hedonistic, power, family prestige and health. Hence the hypothesis of significance of difference in the values of rural and urban students (*i.e.* in chapter 4) was confirmed.

Table 6.14 clearly reveals that arts rural and science rural students vary significantly in respect to their mean scores on all the values except the religious (t=0.01), and the hedonistic (t=0.32) values. It appears proper to say that science students having rural background were found to have more social, democratic, power, aesthetic, family prestige and health values while their arts rural counterparts were having more economic and knowledge values. Hence the hypothesis (*i.e.* in chapter 4) was partly accepted and partly rejected.

Table - 6.15
Comparison of Science Rural and Commerce Rural Students on Values

		Science Rural N=100		Commerce Rural N=90		
Sl.	Values	M	SD	M	SD	t-value
1.	Religious (A)	50.26	9.29	49.23	9.15	0.77
2.	Social (B)	60.15	10.26	45.16	9.20	10.62**
3.	Democratic (C)	63.19	12.50	52.16	10.25	6.68**
4.	Aesthetic (D)	59.16	11.92	49.52	9.69	6.43**
5.	Economic (E)	48.96	9.25	50.16	9.24	0.89
6.	Knowledge (F)	46.19	9.23	46.12	8.50	0.05
7.	Hedonistic (G)	55.16	10.29	42.90	7.31	9.54**
8.	Power (H)	51.28	9.24	45.36	8.32	4.65**
9.	Family Prestige (I)	54.16	10.60	48.19	10.26	3.94**
10.	Health (J)	49.26	10.23	44.16	9.79	3.51**

* P<0.05

** P<0.01

Table 6.15 shows that rural students belonging to science and commerce academic streams differed significantly with respect to seven values, namely social, democratic, aesthetic, hedonistic, power, family prestige and health. It may be noted that the rural students of science stream yielded significantly higher scores on all these seven values. In the rest three values (*i.e.* religious, economic and knowledge) the differences between the two groups were found not to be significant; thus the two groups occupied the similar position in religious, economic and knowledge values. Hence the hypothesis (*i.e.* in chapter 4) was partly accepted and partly rejected.

Table-6.16
Comparison of Arts Rural and Commerce Rural Students on Values

		Arts Rural N=150		Commerce Rural N=90		
Sl.	Values	M	SD	M	SD	t-value
1.	Religious (A)	50.28	9.23	49.23	9.15	0.86
2.	Social (B)	52.25	10.16	45.16	9.20	5.56**
3.	Democratic (C)	49.15	11.34	52.16	10.25	2.11*
4.	Aesthetic (D)	48.29	10.62	49.52	9.69	0.92
5.	Economic (E)	54.26	12.26	50.16	9.24	2.94**
6.	Knowledge (F)	58.15	14.61	46.12	8.50	8.06**
7.	Hedonistic (G)	55.60	11.19	42.90	7.31	10.63**
8.	Power (H)	43.21	9.15	45.36	8.32	1.41
9.	Family Prestige (I)	46.62	10.21	48.19	10.26	1.15
10.	Health (J)	44.18	9.65	44.16	9.79	0.01

* $P<0.05$
** $P<0.01$

When arts rural and commerce rural students were compared with respect to their values (cf Table 6.16), they have shown significant variations in the values like social ($t=5.56$, $p<.01$), democratic ($t=2.11$, $p<.05$), economic ($t=2.94$, $p<.01$), knowledge ($t=8.06$, $p<.01$) and hedonistic ($t=10.63$, $p<.01$). The arts rural students had scored higher mean on social, economic, knowledge and hedonistic values than the commerce rural students. On the other hand, the commerce rural students scored higher mean on democratic values in comparison to the arts rural students. Thus the hypothesis (*i.e.* in chapter 4) was partly retained and partly rejected.

Table - 6.17
Comparison of Arts Urban and Science Urban Students on Values

		Arts Urban N=150		Science Urban N=200		
Sl.	Values	M	SD	M	SD	t-value
1.	Religious (A)	52.42	12.91	60.52	12.20	5.95**
2.	Social (B)	45.32	10.21	65.28	11.29	17.30**
3.	Democratic (C)	55.69	9.23	71.29	13.24	12.98**
4.	Aesthetic (D)	46.28	8.24	72.53	14.26	21.66**
5.	Economic (E)	36.92	7.81	68.25	12.98	27.97**
6.	Knowledge (F)	45.18	8.23	70.20	10.18	26.20**
7.	Hedonistic (G)	50.21	7.29	65.29	9.16	17.14**
8.	Power (H)	49.10	10.27	66.10	10.23	15.35**
9.	Family Prestige (I)	51.28	11.29	69.16	11.69	14.44**
10.	Health (J)	46.92	8.25	60.52	10.91	13.31**

* P<0.05
** P<0.01

An inspection of Table 6.17 would reveal that arts students having urban background differed significantly from their science urban counterparts on all values, namely religious (t=5.95, p<.01), social (t=17.3, p<.01), democratic (t=12.98, p<.01),aesthetic (t=21.66, p<.01), economic (t=27.97, p<.01), knowledge (t=26.2, p<.01), hedonistic (t=17.14, p<.01), power (t=14.44, p<.01), family prestige (t=14.44, p<.01) and health (t=13.31, p<.01). It may be noted that science students having urban background yielded significantly higher values on all values scales. Hence the hypothesis in chapter 4 was retained.

It can be seen from Table 6.18 that as many as eight 't'-values were significant. The 't'-values between science and commerce students belonging to urban area for religious (t=4.11, p<.01), Social (t=4.65, p<.01), democratic (t=10.37, p<.01), aesthetic (t=7.59, p<.01), economic (t=9.02, p<.01), knowledge (t=9.24, p<.01), family prestige (t=14.5, p<.01) and health (t=12.33, p<.01) were statistically significant which tend to imply significant differences in religious, social, democratic, aesthetic, knowledge, family prestige and health values between these two groups. It may be noted that science students having urban background yielded significantly higher values on social, democratic, aesthetic, economic, knowledge, family prestige and health scales than their commerce urban counterparts, while commerce students having urban background indicated significantly higher values on religious scale. The two groups did not differ significantly in the hedonistic and power values. Hence, the hypothesis in chapter 4 was partly accepted and partly rejected.

Table - 6.18
Comparison of Science Urban and Commerce Urban Students on Values

		Science Urban N=200		Commerce Urban N=210		
Sl.	Values	M	SD	M	SD	t-value
1.	Religious (A)	60.52	12.20	65.29	11.23	4.11**
2.	Social (B)	65.28	11.29	60.17	10.93	4.65**
3.	Democratic (C)	71.29	13.24	59.28	9.89	10.37**
4.	Aesthetic (D)	72.53	14.26	63.28	9.91	7.59**
5.	Economic (E)	68.25	12.98	58.51	8.26	9.02**
6.	Knowledge (F)	70.20	10.18	65.29	9.53	9.24**
7.	Hedonistic (G)	65.29	9.16	64.28	8.91	1.13
8.	Power (H)	66.10	10.23	67.51	6.91	1.60
9.	Family Prestige (I)	69.16	11.69	55.21	7.59	14.50**
10.	Health (J)	60.52	10.91	48.69	8.26	12.33**

* P<0.05
** P<0.01

The results as projected in Table 6.19 conclude that arts and commerce students belonging to urban areas differed significantly on all the ten values. The commerce students having urban background had shown higher mean scores on all the ten values than their arts urban counterparts. Therefore, the hypothesis in chapter 4 was accepted.

Table - 6.19
Comparison of Arts Urban and Commerce Urban Students on Values

		Arts Urban N=150		Commerce Urban N=210		
Sl.	Values	M	SD	M	SD	t-value
1.	Religious (A)	52.42	12.91	65.29	11.23	9.85**
2.	Social (B)	45.32	10.21	60.17	10.93	13.21**
3.	Democratic (C)	55.69	9.23	59.28	9.89	3.54**
4.	Aesthetic (D)	46.28	8.24	63.28	9.91	17.72**
5.	Economic (E)	36.92	7.81	58.51	8.26	25.24**
6.	Knowledge (F)	45.18	8.23	65.29	9.53	21.39**
7.	Hedonistic (G)	50.21	7.29	64.28	8.91	16.44**
8.	Power (H)	49.10	10.27	67.51	6.91	19.08**
9.	Family Prestige (I)	51.28	11.29	55.21	7.59	3.71**
10.	Health (J)	46.92	8.25	48.69	8.26	2.01*

* P<0.05
** P<0.01

Table - 6.20
Comparison of Science Urban and Science Rural Students on Values

		Science Urban N=200		Science Rural N=100		
Sl.	Values	M	SD	M	SD	t-value
1.	Religious (A)	60.52	12.20	50.26	9.29	8.09**
2.	Social (B)	65.28	11.29	60.15	10.26	3.95**
3.	Democratic (C)	71.29	13.24	63.19	12.50	5.19**
4.	Aesthetic (D)	72.53	14.26	59.16	11.92	8.56**
5.	Economic (E)	68.25	12.98	48.96	9.25	4.80**
6.	Knowledge (F)	70.20	10.18	46.19	9.23	20.51**
7.	Hedonistic (G)	65.29	9.16	55.16	10.29	8.33**
8.	Power (H)	66.10	10.23	51.28	9.24	12.63**
9.	Family Prestige (I)	69.16	11.69	54.16	10.60	11.16**
10.	Health (J)	60.52	10.91	49.26	10.23	8.79**

* P<.05
** P<.01

Table - 6.21
Comparison of Arts Urban and Arts Rural Students on Values

		Arts Urban N=150		Arts Rural N=150		
Sl.	Values	M	SD	M	SD	t-value
1.	Religious (A)	52.42	12.91	50.28	9.23	1.65
2.	Social (B)	45.32	10.21	52.25	10.16	5.89**
3.	Democratic (C)	55.69	9.23	49.15	11.34	5.48**
4.	Aesthetic (D)	46.28	8.24	48.29	10.62	1.83
5.	Economic (E)	36.92	7.81	54.26	12.26	14.61**
6.	Knowledge (F)	45.18	8.23	58.15	14.61	9.47**
7.	Hedonistic (G)	50.21	7.29	55.60	11.19	4.94**
8.	Power (H)	49.10	10.27	43.21	9.15	5.24**
9.	Family Prestige (I)	51.28	11.29	46.62	10.21	3.75**
10.	Health (J)	46.92	8.25	44.18	9.65	2.65**

* P<.05
** P<.01

Table - 6.22
Comparison of Commmerce Urban and Commerce Rural Students on Values

		Commerce Urban N=210		Commerce Rural N=90		
Sl.	Values	M	SD	M	SD	t-value
1.	Religious (A)	65.29	11.23	49.23	9.15	12.98**
2.	Social (B)	60.17	10.93	45.16	9.20	12.22**
3.	Democratic (C)	59.28	9.89	52.16	10.25	5.57**
4.	Aesthetic (D)	63.28	9.91	49.52	9.69	11.20**
5.	Economic (E)	58.51	8.26	50.16	9.24	7.40**
6.	Knowledge (F)	65.29	9.53	46.12	8.50	17.25**
7.	Hedonistic (G)	64.28	8.91	42.90	7.31	21.68**
8.	Power (H)	67.51	6.91	45.36	8.32	22.18**
9.	Family Prestige (I)	55.21	7.59	48.19	10.26	5.84**
10.	Health (J)	48.69	8.26	44.16	9.79	3.84**

* P<.05
** P<.01

Table - 6.23
Comparison of Science Urban and Arts Rural Students on Values

		Science Urban N=200		Arts Rural N=150		
Sl.	Values	M	SD	M	SD	t-value
1.	Religious (A)	60.52	12.20	50.28	9.23	8.94**
2.	Social (B)	65.28	11.29	52.25	10.16	9.61**
3.	Democratic (C)	71.29	13.24	49.15	11.34	16.81**
4.	Aesthetic (D)	72.53	14.26	48.29	10.62	18.23**
5.	Economic (E)	68.25	12.98	54.26	12.26	10.30**
6.	Knowledge (F)	70.20	10.18	58.15	14.61	8.65**
7.	Hedonistic (G)	65.29	9.16	55.60	11.19	9.69**
8.	Power (H)	66.10	10.23	43.21	9.15	22.01**
9.	Family Prestige (I)	69.16	11.69	46.62	10.21	19.20**
10.	Health (J)	60.52	10.91	44.18	9.65	14.82**

* P<.05
** P<.01

Table - 6.24
Comparison of Science Urban and Commerce Rural Students on Values

		Science Urban N=200		Commerce Rural N=90		
Sl.	Values	M	SD	M	SD	t-value
1.	Religious (A)	60.52	12.20	49.23	9.15	8.72**
2.	Social (B)	65.28	11.29	45.16	9.20	16.01**
3.	Democratic (C)	71.29	13.24	52.16	10.25	13.38**
4.	Aesthetic (D)	72.53	14.26	49.52	9.69	16.03**
5.	Economic (E)	68.25	12.98	50.16	9.24	13.52**
6.	Knowledge (F)	70.20	10.18	46.12	8.50	20.95**
7.	Hedonistic (G)	65.29	9.16	42.90	7.31	22.25**
8.	Power (H)	66.10	10.23	45.36	8.32	18.24**
9.	Family Prestige (I)	69.16	11.69	48.19	10.26	15.40**
10.	Health (J)	60.52	10.91	44.16	9.79	12.68**

* P<.05
** P<.01

Table - 6.25
Comparison of Arts Urban and Science Rural Students on Values

		Arts Urban N=150		Science Rural N=100		
Sl.	Values	M	SD	M	SD	t-value
1.	Religious (A)	52.42	12.91	50.26	9.29	1.54
2.	Social (B)	45.32	10.21	60.15	10.26	11.22**
3.	Democratic (C)	55.69	9.23	63.19	12.50	5.14**
4.	Aesthetic (D)	46.28	8.24	59.16	11.92	9.23**
5.	Economic (E)	36.92	7.81	48.96	9.25	10.72**
6.	Knowledge (F)	45.18	8.23	46.19	9.23	0.86
7.	Hedonistic (G)	50.21	7.29	55.16	10.29	4.17**
8.	Power (H)	49.10	10.27	51.28	9.24	1.75
9.	Family Prestige (I)	51.28	11.29	54.16	10.60	2.05*
10.	Health (J)	46.92	8.25	49.26	10.23	1.91

* P<.05
** P<.01

Table - 6.26
Comparison of Arts Urban and Commerce Rural Students on Values

		Arts Urban N=150		Comm. Rural N=90		
Sl.	Values	M	SD	M	SD	t-value
1.	Religious (A)	52.42	12.91	49.23	9.15	2.23*
2.	Social (B)	45.32	10.21	45.16	9.20	0.12
3.	Democratic (C)	55.69	9.23	52.16	10.25	2.68**
4.	Aesthetic (D)	46.28	8.24	49.52	9.69	2.65**
5.	Economic (E)	36.92	7.81	50.16	9.24	11.37**
6.	Knowledge (F)	45.18	8.23	46.12	8.50	0.83
7.	Hedonistic (G)	50.21	7.29	42.90	7.31	7.51**
8.	Power (H)	49.10	10.27	45.36	8.32	3.08**
9.	Family Prestige (I)	51.28	11.29	48.19	10.26	2.17*
10.	Health (J)	46.92	8.25	44.16	9.79	2.24*

* P<.05
** P<.01

The results of the comparison of science students having urban and rural background on values are shown in Table 6.20. It can be noticed that the two groups differed significantly in all the ten values. On the basis of the comparison of mean scores it was found that the science students having urban background yielded significantly higher scores on all the ten values. Hence the hypothesis in chapter 4 anticipating significant difference in values of both the groups was accepted.

It can be observed from Table 6.21 that arts students having urban and rural background differed significantly in respect to their mean scores on all the values except the religious (t=1.65) and aesthetic (t=1.83) values. It seems proper to say that arts students having urban background were found to have more democratic (M=55.69), power (M=49.1), family prestige (M=51.28), and health (M=46.92) values while their rural counterparts were having more social (M=52.25), economic (M=54.26), knowledge (M=58.15) and hedonistic (M=55.6) values. Hence the research hypothesis in chapter 4 was partly accepted and partly rejected.

The results as projected in Table 6.22 conclude that commerce students having rural-urban background differed significantly on all the ten values. The commerce students having urban background had shown higher mean scores on all the ten values than their rural counterparts. Hence the hypothesis in chapter 4 was confirmed.

Table 6.23 presents results pertaining to the significance of difference between means of science students having urban background and arts students having rural background on ten different values. It may be observed that the two groups differed significantly in all the ten values. The science students having urban background exhibited significantly higher values on all the scales than their arts rural counterparts. Hence the hypothesis in chapter 4 of significance of difference in values of science urban and arts rural students stood confirmed.

It can be concluded from the results presented in Table 6.24 that science students having urban background and commerce students having rural background differed significantly on all the ten values. The science students having urban background had shown higher mean scores on all the ten values than their commerce rural counterparts. Hence the hypothesis in chapter 4 was retained.

The statistical analysis (vide Table 6.25) revealed that arts students having urban background and science students having rural background differed significantly in respect to their mean scores on six values Social, (t=11.22, p<.01), democratic (t=5.14, p<.01), aesthetic

Table - 6.27
Comparison of Commmerce Urban and Science Rural Students on Values

		Commerce Urban N=210		Science Rural N=100		
Sl.	Values	M	SD	M	SD	t-value
1.	Religious (A)	65.29	11.23	50.26	9.29	12.42**
2.	Social (B)	60.17	10.93	60.15	10.26	0.01
3.	Democratic (C)	59.28	9.89	63.19	12.50	2.74**
4.	Aesthetic (D)	63.28	9.91	59.16	11.92	2.99**
5.	Economic (E)	58.51	8.26	48.96	9.25	8.79**
6.	Knowledge (F)	65.29	9.54	46.19	9.23	16.85**
7.	Hedonistic (G)	64.28	8.91	55.16	10.29	7.61**
8.	Power (H)	67.51	6.91	51.28	9.24	15.61**
9.	Family Prestige (I)	55.21	7.59	54.16	10.60	0.89
10.	Health (J)	48.69	8.26	49.26	10.23	0.49

* P<.05
** P<.01

Table - 6.28
Comparison of Commmerce Urban and Arts Rural Students on Values

		Commerce Urban N=210		Arts Rural N=150		
Sl.	Values	M	SD	M	SD	t-value
1.	Religious (A)	65.29	11.23	50.28	9.23	13.89**
2.	Social (B)	60.17	10.93	52.25	10.16	7.13**
3.	Democratic (C)	59.28	9.89	49.15	11.34	8.81**
4.	Aesthetic (D)	63.28	9.91	48.29	10.62	13.58**
5.	Economic (E)	58.51	8.26	54.26	12.26	3.69**
6.	Knowledge (F)	65.29	9.53	58.15	14.61	5.24**
7.	Hedonistic (G)	64.28	8.91	55.60	11.19	7.88**
8.	Power (H)	67.51	6.91	43.21	9.15	27.42**
9.	Family Prestige (I)	55.21	7.59	46.62	10.21	8.73**
10.	Health (J)	48.69	8.26	44.18	9.65	4.64**

* P<.05
** P<.01

Table - 6.29
Comparison of Male and Female Students on Values

		Male N=615		Female N=285		
Sl.	Values	M	SD	M	SD	t-value
1.	Religious (A)	44.85	9.26	43.87	7.44	1.69
2.	Social (B)	22.38	9.13	23.88	9.63	2.21*
3.	Democratic (C)	37.50	8.23	37.53	8.02	0.05
4.	Aesthetic (D)	55.49	10.46	52.95	9.26	3.67**
5.	Economic (E)	55.49	12.01	59.32	9.62	5.12**
6.	Knowledge (F)	39.61	9.00	40.06	9.48	0.67
7.	Hedonistic (G)	65.36	7.56	62.35	9.17	4.83**
8.	Power (H)	68.65	7.25	61.49	10.72	10.24
9.	Family Prestige (I)	51.08	7.88	48.34	8.57	4.57**
10.	Health (J)	36.69	7.00	35.49	7.66	2.24*

* P<.05
** P<.01

Table - 6.30
Comparison of Arts Male and Science Male Students on Values

		Arts Male N=180		Science Male N=210		
Sl.	Values	M	SD	M	SD	t-value
1.	Religious (A)	43.83	9.34	46.10	9.60	2.36*
2.	Social (B)	23.16	9.25	22.97	8.76	0.21
3.	Democratic (C)	38.13	7.95	36.59	7.96	1.91
4.	Aesthetic (D)	54.15	11.59	56.35	9.57	2.02*
5.	Economic (E)	53.06	11.96	57.12	11.92	3.35**
6.	Knowledge (F)	37.84	8.37	40.90	9.07	3.46**
7.	Hedonistic (G)	64.83	7.34	63.66	7.76	1.53
8.	Power (H)	68.14	7.00	67.97	8.04	0.23
9.	Family Prestige (I)	52.52	7.41	52.29	7.68	0.31
10.	Health (J)	35.50	6.07	38.03	7.51	3.68**

* P<.05
** P<.01

(t=9.23, p<.01), economic (t=10.72, p<.01), hedonistic (t=4.17, p<.01) and family prestige (t=2.05, p<.05). It may be noted that science students having rural background yielded significantly higher values on all those six scales namely social, democratic, aesthetic, economic, hedonistic and family prestige, than their arts urban counterparts. However both the groups occupied the similar position in case of the remaining four values (*i.e.* religious, knowledge, power an health). Hence the research hypothesis in chapter 4 was partly accepted and partly rejected.

An inspection of Table 6.26 revealed significance of difference between the mean scores of arts students having urban bcakground and commerce students having rural background on values like religious (t=2.23, p<.05), democratic (t=2.68, p<.01), aesthetic (t=2.65, p<.01), economic (t=11.37, p<.01), hedonistic (t=7.51, p<.01), power (t=3.08, p<.01), family prestige (t=2.17, p<.05) and health (t=2.24, p<.05). This suggests that these two groups of students differed significantly with respect to their religious, democratic, aesthetic, economic, hedonistic, power, family prestige and health values. It may be noted that arts students having urban background yielded significantly higher values on religious, democratic, hedonistic, power, family prestige and health scales than their commerce rural counterparts, while the commerce students having rural background indicated significantly higher values on aesthetic and economic scales than their arts urban counterparts. The two groups however, did not differ significantly in social and knowledge values. Hence the hypothesis in chapter 4 was partly accepted and partly rejected.

Table 6.27 shows that urban students belonging to commerce stream and rural students belonging to science stream differed significantly with respect to seven values, namely religious democratic, aesthetic economic, knowledge, hedonistic and power. It may be noted that the urban students belonging to commerce stream yielded significantly higher values on religious, aesthetic, economic, knowledge, hedonistic and power scales than their science rural counterparts, while the rural students belonging to science stream yielded significantly higher value on democratic scale than their commerce urban counterparts. The two groups, however, occupied the similar position in social, family prestige, and health values. Hence the hypothesis in chapter 4 was partly accepted and partly rejected.

It can be concluded from the results presented in Table 6.28 that commerce students having urban background and arts students having rural background differed significantly on all the ten values. The

Table - 6.31
Comparison of Science Male and Commerce Male Students on Values

		Science Male N=210		Commerce Male N=225		
Sl.	Values	M	SD	M	SD	t-value
1.	Religious (A)	46.10	9.60	44.61	8.83	1.68
2.	Social (B)	22.97	8.76	21.00	9.37	2.27*
3.	Democratic (C)	36.59	7.96	37.77	8.77	1.47
4.	Aesthetic (D)	56.35	9.57	55.97	10.22	0.40
5.	Economic (E)	57.12	11.92	56.28	12.14	0.73
6.	Knowledge (F)	40.90	9.07	40.10	9.57	0.89
7.	Hedonistic (G)	63.66	7.76	67.60	7.59	5.35**
8.	Power (H)	67.97	8.04	69.84	6.71	2.62**
9.	Family Prestige (I)	52.29	7.68	48.44	8.55	4.98**
10.	Health (J)	38.03	7.51	36.55	7.43	2.06*

* P<.05
** P<.01

Table - 6.32
Comparison of Arts Male and Commerce Male Students on Values

		Arts Male N=180		Commerce Female N=225		
Sl.	Values	M	SD	M	SD	t-value
1.	Religious (A)	43.83	9.34	44.61	8.83	0.85
2.	Social (B)	23.16	9.25	21.00	9.37	2.32*
3.	Democratic (C)	38.13	7.95	37.77	8.77	0.52
4.	Aesthetic (D)	54.15	11.59	55.97	10.22	1.65
5.	Economic (E)	53.06	11.96	56.28	12.14	2.68**
6.	Knowledge (F)	37.84	8.37	40.10	9.57	2.54*
7.	Hedonistic (G)	64.83	7.34	67.60	7.59	3.72**
8.	Power (H)	68.14	7.00	69.84	6.71	2.47**
9.	Family Prestige (I)	52.52	7.41	48.44	8.55	5.14**
10.	Health (J)	35.50	6.07	36.55	7.43	1.56

* P<.05
** P<.01

commerce students having urban background had shown higher mean scores on all the ten values than their arts rural counterparts. hence the hypothesis in chapter 4 was accepted.

COMPARISON OF VALUES OF MALE AND FEMALE STUDENTS

In pursuance of the objective in chapter 4 of the study 'to compare the values of higher secondary male and female students', significance of difference between relevant means were tested by employing 't'-tests. The obtained results have been presented below in order to test the concerned hypothesis.

The results of analysis with regard to significance of difference in means of students' personal values for male and female students together with various subgroups are presented in Tables 6.29 through 6.44.

Table 6.29 summarizes the results pertaining to the significance of difference between means of male and female students on values. From Table 6.29, one may gather that the seven 't'- values for groupings based on sex of students (*i.e.* social, t=2.21, p<.05, aesthetic, t=3.67, p<.01; economic, t=5.12, p<.01; hedonistic, t=4.83, p<.01; power, t=10.24, p<.01; family prestige, t=4.57, p<.01; and health t=2.24, p<.05) were found to be significant. Results revealed that the male students had scored significantly higher mean scores on aesthetic, hedonistic, power, family prestige and health values than their female counterparts. On the other hand the female students indicated significantly higher values on social and economic scales. However the two groups did not differ significantly in religious, democratic and knowledge values. Hence the hypothesis in chapter 4 "there will significant difference in the values of male and female students" was partly accepted in those seven values where significant difference was noted and partly rejected in those three values where significant difference was not noted.

Table 6.30 shows the results of the application of 't'-test for the differences obtained by arts male and science male students on values. It may be noted that science male students yielded significantly higher values on all the five scales, namely religious (M=46.1), aesthetic (M=56.35), economic (M=57.12), knowledge (M=40.9) and health (M=38.03). In all these five values the differences between the two groups were found to be significant. However, the two groups did not differ significantly in social, democratic, hedonistic, power and family prestige values. In view of these results, the hypothesis in chapter 4 was partly accepted and partly rejected.

Table - 6.33
Comparison of Arts Female and Science Female Students on Values

		Arts Female N=120		Science Female N=90		
Sl.	Values	M	SD	M	SD	t-value
1.	Religious (A)	44.97	7.30	44.54	8.19	0.39
2.	Social (B)	26.63	8.77	21.92	10.33	3.52**
3.	Democratic (C)	39.02	8.08	36.31	8.79	2.29*
4.	Aesthetic (D)	53.37	9.73	50.06	9.78	2.43*
5.	Economic (E)	59.54	9.09	57.08	10.77	1.75
6.	Knowledge (F)	41.92	8.83	39.03	9.45	2.25*
7.	Hedonistic (G)	63.10	8.82	60.42	9.17	2.13*
8.	Power (H)	62.68	9.90	56.08	12.76	4.07**
9.	Family Prestige (I)	49.65	9.14	46.04	8.80	2.89**
10.	Health (J)	37.24	8.09	35.41	7.02	1.75

* P<.05
** P<.01

Table - 6.34
Comparison of Science Female and Commerce Female Students on Values

		Science Female N=90		Commerce Female N=75		
Sl.	Values	M	SD	M	SD	t-value
1.	Religious (A)	44.54	8.19	42.11	6.85	2.07*
2.	Social (B)	21.92	10.33	23.10	9.91	0.75
3.	Democratic (C)	36.31	8.79	37.25	7.20	0.76
4.	Aesthetic (D)	50.06	9.78	54.83	8.28	3.39**
5.	Economic (E)	57.08	10.77	61.33	9.11	2.77**
6.	Knowledge (F)	39.03	9.45	39.23	10.17	0.12
7.	Hedonistic (G)	60.42	9.17	63.52	9.53	2.11*
8.	Power (H)	56.08	12.76	65.71	9.52	5.54**
9.	Family Prestige (I)	46.04	8.80	49.33	7.77	2.59**
10.	Health (J)	35.41	7.02	33.83	7.87	1.35

* P<.05
** P<.01

Table - 6.35
Comparison of Arts Female and Commerce Female Students on Values

		Arts Female N=120		Commerce Female N=75		
Sl.	Values	M	SD	M	SD	t-value
1.	Religious (A)	44.97	7.30	42.11	6.85	2.76**
2.	Social (B)	26.63	8.77	23.10	9.91	2.53*
3.	Democratic (C)	39.02	8.08	37.25	7.20	1.59
4.	Aesthetic (D)	53.37	9.73	54.83	8.28	1.14
5.	Economic (E)	59.54	9.09	61.33	9.11	1.34
6.	Knowledge (F)	41.92	8.83	39.23	10.17	1.89
7.	Hedonistic (G)	63.10	8.82	63.52	9.53	0.31
8.	Power (H)	62.68	9.90	65.71	9.52	2.17*
9.	Family Prestige (I)	49.65	9.14	49.33	7.77	0.26
10.	Health (J)	37.24	8.09	33.83	7.87	4.23**

* P<.05
** P<.01

Table - 6.36
Comparison of Science Male and Science Female Students on Values

		Science Male N=210		Science Female N=90		
Sl.	Values	M	SD	M	SD	t-value
1.	Religious (A)	46.10	9.60	44.54	8.19	1.43
2.	Social (B)	22.97	8.76	21.92	10.33	0.84
3.	Democratic (C)	36.59	7.96	36.31	8.79	0.26
4.	Aesthetic (D)	56.35	9.57	50.06	9.78	5.14**
5.	Economic (E)	57.12	11.92	57.08	10.77	0.03
6.	Knowledge (F)	40.90	9.07	39.03	9.45	1.59
7.	Hedonistic (G)	63.66	7.76	60.42	9.17	2.93**
8.	Power (H)	67.97	8.04	56.08	12.76	8.17**
9.	Family Prestige (I)	52.29	7.68	46.04	8.80	5.84**
10.	Health (J)	38.03	7.51	35.41	7.02	2.90**

* P<.05
** P<.01

Table - 6.37
Comparison of Arts Male and Arts Female Students on Values

		Arts Male N=180		Arts Female N=120		
Sl.	Values	M	SD	M	SD	t-value
1.	Religious (A)	43.83	9.34	44.97	7.30	1.18
2.	Social (B)	23.16	9.25	26.63	8.77	3.28**
3.	Democratic (C)	38.13	7.95	39.02	8.08	0.94
4.	Aesthetic (D)	54.15	11.59	53.37	9.73	0.63
5.	Economic (E)	53.06	11.96	59.54	9.09	5.32**
6.	Knowledge (F)	37.84	8.37	41.92	8.83	4.00**
7.	Hedonistic (G)	64.83	7.34	63.10	8.82	1.77
8.	Power (H)	68.14	7.00	62.68	9.90	5.23**
9.	Family Prestige (I)	52.52	7.41	49.65	9.14	2.87**
10.	Health (J)	35.50	6.07	37.24	8.09	2.01*

* P<.05
** P<.01

Table - 6.38
Comparison of Commerce Male and Commerce Female Students on Values

		Commerce Male N=225		Commerce Female N=75		
Sl.	Values	M	SD	M	SD	t-value
1.	Religious (A)	44.61	8.83	42.11	6.85	2.53*
2.	Social (B)	21.00	9.37	23.10	9.91	1.61
3.	Democratic (C)	37.77	8.77	37.25	7.20	0.51
4.	Aesthetic (D)	55.97	10.22	54.83	8.28	0.97
5.	Economic (E)	56.28	12.14	61.33	9.11	3.80**
6.	Knowledge (F)	40.10	9.57	39.23	10.17	0.65
7.	Hedonistic (G)	67.60	7.59	63.52	9.53	3.37**
8.	Power (H)	69.84	6.17	65.71	9.52	3.48**
9.	Family Prestige (I)	48.44	8.55	49.33	7.77	0.84
10.	Health (J)	36.55	7.43	33.83	7.87	2.63**

* P≤.05
** P<.01

Table-6.39
Comparison of Science Male and Arts Female Students on Values

		Science Male N=210		Arts Female N=120		
Sl.	Values	M	SD	M	SD	t-value
1.	Religious (A)	46.10	9.60	44.97	7.30	1.20
2.	Social (B)	22.97	8.76	26.63	8.77	3.65**
3.	Democratic (C)	36.59	7.96	39.02	8.08	2.44*
4.	Aesthetic (D)	56.35	9.57	53.37	9.73	2.69**
5.	Economic (E)	57.12	11.92	59.54	9.09	2.09*
6.	Knowledge (F)	40.90	9.07	41.92	8.83	1.00
7.	Hedonistic (G)	63.66	7.76	63.10	8.82	0.58
8.	Power (H)	67.97	8.04	62.68	9.90	4.99**
9.	Family Prestige (I)	52.29	7.68	49.65	9.14	2.67**
10.	Health (J)	38.03	7.51	37.24	8.09	0.87

* P<.05
** P<.01

Table - 6.40
Comparison of Science Male and Commerce Female Students on Values

		Science Male N=210		Commerce Female N=75		
Sl.	Values	M	SD	M	SD	t-value
1.	Religious (A)	46.10	9.60	42.11	6.85	3.87**
2.	Social (B)	22.97	8.76	23.10	9.91	0.10
3.	Democratic (C)	36.59	7.96	37.25	7.20	0.66
4.	Aesthetic (D)	56.35	9.57	54.83	8.28	1.31
5.	Economic (E)	57.12	11.92	61.33	9.11	3.15**
6.	Knowledge (F)	40.90	9.07	39.23	10.17	1.25
7.	Hedonistic (G)	63.66	7.76	63.52	9.53	0.11
8.	Power (H)	67.97	8.04	65.71	9.52	1.84
9.	Family Prestige (I)	52.29	7.68	49.33	7.77	2.84**
10.	Health (J)	38.03	7.51	33.83	7.87	4.01**

* P<.05
** P<.01

Table 6.31 discloses that only five 't'- values were significant. This suggests that science and commerce male students differed significantly with respect to social (t=2.27, p<.05), hedonistic (t=5.35, p<.01), power (t=2.62, p<.01), family prestige (t=4.98, p<.01) and health (t=2.06, p<.05) values. Further, greater mean scores in social, family prestige and health values were in favour of science male students, which implies that science male students had significantly higher level of social, family prestige and health values than their commerce male counterparts. On the other hand the commerce male students indicated significantly higher values on hedonistic and power values. Both the groups, however, occupied the similar position in case of religious, democratic aesthetic, economic and knowledge values. In view of the mixed results the hypothesis in chapter 4 was partly accepted and partly rejected.

It is evident from Table 6.32 that significant differences existed in mean scores of arts and commerce male students with respect to their social, economic, knowledge, hedonistic, power, and family prestige values. The commerce male students appeared to have greater magnitude of economic, knowledge, hedonistic and power values in comparison to arts male students. On the other hand, the arts male students appeared to have greater magnitude of social and family prestige values in comparison to their commerce male counterparts. On rest of the values, arts and commerce male students were found to be alike. Hence the research hypothesis in chapter 4 was partly accepted and partly rejected.

Table 6.33 shows that arts and science female students differed significantly with respect to seven values, namely social, democratic, aesthetic, knowledge, hedonistic, power and family prestice. Further arts female students showed superiority over science female students on all those seven values. On rest of the values arts and science female students were found to be alike. Hence, the research hypothesis in chapter 4 was partly retained and partly rejected.

It can be seen from Table 6.34 that six 't'- values were significant which suggest significant differences in religious, aesthetic, economic, hedonistic, power and family prestige values between science and commerce female students. Further, commerce female students showed superiority over science female students with reference to aesthetic, economic, hedonistic, power and family prestige values. On the other hand science female students exhibited superiority over commerce female students with regard to religious values. Both the groups, however, occupied the similar position in case of social, democratic, knowledge and health values. Hence the hypothesis in chapter 4 was partly accepted and partly rejected.

A close perusal of Table 6.35 revealed significance of four 't'-values (*i.e.* religious, t=2.76, p<.01; social, t=2.53, p<.05; power, t=2.17, p<.05; and health,t=4.23, p<.01) that suggest significant differences in religious, social, power and health values. The arts female students showed superiority over commerce female students with respect to religious, social and health values while the commerce female students exhibited superiority over arts female students on power values. Hence the hypothesis of significant differences in values in chapter 4 was accepted with regard to foregoing four values. However, both the groups were found to be similar with regard to democratic, aesthetic, economic, knowledge, hedonistic and family prestige values. Here the hypothesis in chapter 4 was rejected.

When the male and female students of science stream were compared (vide Table 6.36), it was found that the science male students were having greater magnitude of aesthetic, hedonistic, power, family prestige and health values. In all these five values the differences between the two groups were found to be significant at .01 level of confidence. However, the two groups did not differ significantly in religious, social, democratic, economic, and knowledge values. Hence the hypothesis in chapter 4 was partly accepted and partly rejected.

Significant differences in the value preferences between arts male and female students were noted in the value areas like social (t=3.28, p<.01), economic (t=5.32, p<.01), knowledge (t=4.00, p<.01), power (t=5.23, p<.01),family prestige (t=2.87, p<.01) and health (t=2.01, p<.05) (vide Table 6.37). Both the groups differed significantly in respect of those six values. Hence the hypothesis of significant differences in values in chapter 4 was retained in those areas of value. In terms of their mean value scores, arts females students indicated significantly higher values on social, economic, knowledge and health scales, while arts male students yielded significantly higher values on power and family prestige scales. However the two groups did not differ significantly in religious, democratic, aesthetic and hedonistic values. Here the hypothesis in chapter 4 was rejected.

It is evident from Table 6.38 that excepting social, democratic, aesthetic, knowledge and family prestige values there were significant differences in the value preferences of these two groups (*i.e.* commerce male and female student). So it can be said that commerce male and female students differed significantly in their value preferences, particularly in the values like religious, economic, hedonistic, power

Table - 6.41
Comparison of Arts Male and Science Female Students on Values

		Arts Male N=180		Science Female N=90		
Sl.	Values	M	SD	M	SD	t-value
1.	Religious (A)	43.83	9.34	44.54	8.19	0.64
2.	Social (B)	23.16	9.25	21.92	10.33	0.96
3.	Democratic (C)	38.13	7.95	36.31	8.79	1.65
4.	Aesthetic (D)	54.15	11.59	50.06	9.78	3.04**
5.	Economic (E)	53.06	11.96	57.08	10.77	2.79**
6.	Knowledge (F)	37.84	8.37	39.03	9.45	1.01
7.	Hedonistic (G)	64.83	7.34	60.42	9.17	3.97**
8.	Power (H)	68.14	7.00	56.08	12.76	8.37**
9.	Family Prestige (I)	52.52	7.41	46.04	8.80	6.01**
10.	Health (J)	35.50	6.07	35.41	7.02	0.10

* P<.05
** P<.01

Table - 6.42
Comparison of Arts Male and Commerce Female Students on Values

		Arts Male N=180		Commerce Female N=75		
Sl.	Values	M	SD	M	SD	t-value
1.	Religious (A)	43.83	9.34	42.11	6.85	1.63
2.	Social (B)	23.16	9.25	23.10	9.91	0.04
3.	Democratic (C)	38.13	7.95	37.25	7.20	0.86
4.	Aesthetic (D)	54.15	11.59	54.83	8.28	0.53
5.	Economic (E)	53.06	11.96	61.33	9.11	5.99**
6.	Knowledge (F)	37.84	8.37	39.23	10.17	1.04
7.	Hedonistic (G)	64.83	7.34	63.52	9.53	1.07
8.	Power (H)	68.14	7.00	65.71	9.52	2.00*
9.	Family Prestige (I)	52.52	7.41	49.33	7.77	3.03**
10.	Health (J)	35.50	6.07	33.83	7.87	1.64

* P<.05
** P<.01

Table - 6.43

Comparison of Commerce Male and Science Female Students on Values

		Comm. Male N=225		Science Female N=90		
Sl.	Values	M	SD	M	SD	t-value
1.	Religious (A)	44.61	8.83	44.54	8.19	0.06
2.	Social (B)	21.00	9.37	21.92	10.33	0.73
3.	Democratic (C)	37.77	8.77	36.31	8.79	1.33
4.	Aesthetic (D)	55.97	10.22	50.06	9.78	4.78**
5.	Economic (E)	56.28	12.14	57.08	10.77	0.57
6.	Knowledge (F)	40.10	9.57	39.3	9.45	0.90
7.	Hedonistic (G)	67.60	7.59	60.42	9.17	6.58**
8.	Power (H)	69.84	6.17	56.08	12.76	9.71**
9.	Family Prestige (I)	48.44	8.55	46.04	8.80	2.20*
10.	Health (J)	36.55	7.43	35.41	7.02	1.28

* P<.05
** p<.01

Table - 6.44

Comparison of Commerce Male and Arts Female Students on Values

		Comm. Male N=225		Arts Female N=120		
Sl.	Values	M	SD	M	SD	t-value
1.	Religious (A)	44.61	8.83	44.97	7.30	0.40
2.	Social (B)	21.00	9.37	26.63	8.77	5.55**
3.	Democratic (C)	37.77	8.77	39.02	8.08	1.33
4.	Aesthetic (D)	55.97	10.22	53.37	9.73	2.32*
5.	Economic (E)	56.28	12.14	59.54	9.09	2.81**
6.	Knowledge (F)	40.10	9.57	41.92	8.83	1.77
7.	Hedonistic (G)	67.60	7.59	63.10	8.82	4.73**
8.	Power (H)	69.84	6.17	62.68	9.90	7.10**
9.	Family Prestige (I)	48.44	8.55	49.65	9.14	1.20
10.	Health (J)	36.55	7.43	37.24	8.09	0.74

* P<.05
** P<.01

and health. It may be observed that commerce male students scored significantly high on religious, hedonistic, power and health values while commerce female students demonstrated significantly higher scores on economic values. In view of these results the hypothesis in chapter 4 was partly accepted and partly rejected.

Table 6.39 reveals that the obtained 't'-values for social, democratic, aesthetic, economic, power and family prestige values were found to be significant as the research hypothesis in chapter 4 got accepted. This observation leads to the inference that the science male and arts female students differed significantly with each other in their social, democratic, aesthetic, economic, power and family prestige values. It may be observed that science male students scored significantly high on aesthetic, power and family prestige values while arts female students exhibited significantly higher scores on social, democratic and economic values. However the two groups did not differ significantly in religious knowledge, hedonistic and health values. Here the hypothesis in chapter 4 was rejected.

Table 6.40 shows that science male and commerce female students differed significantly only in four values namely religious, economic, family prestige and health. The hypothesis in chapter 4 was accepted and differences were found to be significant at .01 level of confidence. It may be noted that science male students yielded significantly higher values on religious, family prestige and health scales while the commerce female students indicated significantly higher values on economic scale. However, both the groups occupied the similar position in case of social, democratic, aesthetic, knowledge, hedonistic and power values. Hence here the hypothesis in chapter 4 was rejected.

From Table 6.41 it may be observed that the 't'- values for aesthetic, economic, hedonistic, power and family prestige values were reported to be significant at .01 level of confidence. The research hypothesis in chapter 4 was retained at this level. It may be observed that arts male students scored significantly high on aesthetic, hedonistic, power and family prestige values while science female students demonstrated significantly higher score on economic value. On rest of the values (*i.e.* religious, social, democratic, knowledge and health), arts male and science female students were found to be alike. Hence the hypothesis in chapter 4 was rejected here.

Table 6.42 reveals that arts male and commerce female students differed significantly only in three values, namely economic, power and family prestige. The hypothesis in chapter 4 was accepted and differences were found to be significant at .01 level for economic and family prestige values while power values could attain significance only at .05 level of confidence. It may be observed that arts male students yielded significantly higher values on power and family prestige scale, while the commerce female students indicated significantly higher values on economic scale. However, both the groups were found to be similar with regard to religious, social, democratic, aesthetic knowledge and health values. Hence the hypothesis in chapter 4 was rejected here.

An inspection of Table 6.43 would reveal that the obtained 't'-values for aesthetic, hedonistic, power and family prestige values were found to be significant; hence the research hypothesis in chapter 4 stood confirmed. This observation leads to the inference that the commerce male and science female students differed significantly with each other in their aesthetic, hedonistic, power and family prestige values. It may be noted that commerce male students scored significantly higher on all these four values (*i.e.* aesthetic,hedonistic, power and family prestige) than their science female counterparts. However, both the groups were found to be similar with regard to religious. Social, democratic, economic, knowledge and health values. So the hypothesis in chapter 4 was rejected here.

Table 6.44 reveals that commerce male and arts female students differed significantly only in five values, namely social, aesthetic, economic, hedonistic and power. The hypothesis in chapter 4 was accepted and differences were found to be significant at .01 level for social, economic, hedonistic and power values while aesthetic values could attain significance only at .05 level of significance. It may be noted that commerce male students exhibited significantly higher values on aesthetic, hedonistic and power scales, while the arts female students yielded significantly higher values on social and economic scales. However, the two groups did not differ significantly in religious, democratic, knowledge, family prestige and health values and the hypothesis in chapter 4 was rejected here.

COMPARISON OF VALUES OF HIGH AND LOW ACHIEVERS

As discussed earlier, one's values constitute an important source of behavioural motivation. School learning is also an aspect of behaviour. In a few researches attempts have been made to find out the relationship between students' values and academic achievement. In the present study the investigator has made an effort to find out the relationship between values and achievement of higher secondary students.

Table - 6.45
Comparison of High Achievers and Low Achievers on Values

Sl.	Values	High Achievers N=243		Low Achievers N=243		
		M	SD	M	SD	t-value
1.	Religious (A)	45.55	9.20	44.10	10.90	1.56
2.	Social (B)	22.62	9.72	26.24	9.67	4.11**
3.	Democratic (C)	38.34	9.80	37.05	7.16	1.66
4.	Aesthetic (D)	54.59	9.85	54.30	11.15	0.30
5.	Economic (E)	60.12	10.40	53.36	13.25	1.77
6.	Knowledge (F)	39.18	9.93	41.09	10.81	2.03*
7.	Hedonistic (G)	66.14	10.36	62.98	8.94	3.60**
8.	Power (H)	66.75	9.54	64.19	10.98	2.75**
9.	Family Prestige (I)	50.18	8.57	49.93	8.75	0.32
10.	Health (J)	35.72	7.57	35.18	9.48	0.69

* P<.05
** P<.01

Table - 6.46
Comparison of High Achievers of Science and Arts Streams on Values

Sl.	Values	High Achievers (Science) N=81		High Achievers (Arts) N=81		
		M	SD	M	SD	t-value
1.	Religious (A)	46.60	9.76	45.06	6.51	1.18
2.	Social (B)	25.71	9.35	22.28	8.97	2.38**
3.	Democratic (C)	37.38	11.78	40.17	8.32	1.74
4.	Aesthetic (D)	53.46	10.86	52.01	10.35	0.87
5.	Economic (E)	57.55	10.19	60.62	12.30	1.73
6.	Knowledge (F)	37.80	9.56	40.35	8.90	1.70
7.	Hedonistic (G)	63.67	8.89	67.12	9.47	2.39*
8.	Power (H)	64.95	9.24	68.50	8.01	2.61*
9.	Family Prestige (I)	49.90	7.30	51.33	8.08	1.60
10.	Health (J)	35.83	7.09	36.00	7.08	0.15

* P<.05
** P<.01

Table - 6.47
Comparison of High Achievers of Science and Commerce Streams on Values

		High Achievers (Sci.) N=81		High Achievers (Comm.) N=81		
Sl.	Values	M	SD	M	SD	t-value
1.	Religious (A)	46.60	9.76	45.01	11.34	0.96
2.	Social (B)	25.71	9.35	19.88	10.84	3.67**
3.	Democratic (C)	37.38	11.78	37.48	9.32	0.05
4.	Aesthetic (D)	53.46	10.86	58.32	8.35	4.05**
5.	Economic (E)	57.55	10.19	62.20	8.73	3.12**
6.	Knowledge (F)	37.80	9.56	39.39	11.34	0.96
7.	Hedonistic (G)	63.67	8.89	67.65	12.72	2.31*
8.	Power (H)	64.95	9.24	66.81	11.38	1.14
9.	Family Prestige (I)	49.90	7.30	49.83	10.35	0.30
10.	Health (J)	35.83	7.09	35.35	8.54	0.39

* P<.05
** P<.01

Table - 6.48
Comparison of High Achievers of Arts and Commerce Streams on Values

		High Achievers (Arts) N=81		High Achievers (Comm.)N=81		
Sl.	Values	M	SD	M	SD	t-value
1.	Religious (A)	45.06	6.51	45.01	11.34	0.03
2.	Social (B)	22.28	8.97	19.88	10.84	1.53
3.	Democratic (C)	40.17	8.32	37.48	9.32	1.94
4.	Aesthetic (D)	52.01	10.35	58.32	8.35	4.27**
5.	Economic (E)	60.62	12.30	62.20	8.73	0.94
6.	Knowledge (F)	40.35	8.90	39.39	11.34	0.60
7.	Hedonistic (G)	67.12	9.47	67.65	12.72	0.30
8.	Power (H)	68.50	8.01	66.81	11.38	1.09
9.	Family Prestige (I)	51.33	8.08	49.83	10.35	1.03
10.	Health (J)	36.00	7.08	35.35	8.54	0.53

* P<.05
** P<.01

Table - 6.49

Comparison of Low Achievers of Science and Arts Streams on Values

		Low Achievers (Science) N=81		Low Achievers (Arts) N=81		
Sl.	Values	M	SD	M	SD	t-value
1.	Religious (A)	42.33	10.63	45.06	9.53	1.75
2.	Social (B)	25.53	11.57	27.92	9.21	1.45
3.	Democratic (C)	35.54	6.46	37.69	6.74	2.07*
4.	Aesthetic (D)	55.09	7.29	54.29	10.90	0.55
5.	Economic (E)	51.60	15.88	48.44	15.41	1.28
6.	Knowledge (F)	41.67	10.41	41.09	9.18	0.37
7.	Hedonistic (G)	61.46	10.70	65.14	6.99	2.59*
8.	Power (H)	61.41	10.95	63.48	10.45	1.23
9.	Family Prestige (I)	49.93	9.75	51.23	7.10	0.97
10.	Health (J)	37.49	11.23	33.01	8.39	2.88**

* P<.05
** P<.01

Table - 6.50

Comparison of Low Achievers of Science and Commerce Streams on Values

		Low Achievers (Science) N=81		Low Achievers (Comm.)N=81		
Sl.	Values	M	SD	M	SD	t-value
1.	Religious (A)	42.33	10.63	44.93	12.56	1.42
2.	Social (B)	25.53	11.57	25.27	8.24	0.16
3.	Democratic (C)	35.54	6.46	37.92	8.30	2.04*
4.	Aesthetic (D)	55.09	7.29	53.54	15.28	0.82
5.	Economic (E)	51.60	15.88	60.06	8.47	4.23**
6.	Knowledge (F)	41.67	10.41	40.53	12.84	0.62
7.	Hedonistic (G)	61.46	10.70	62.34	9.14	0.56
8.	Power (H)	61.41	10.95	67.70	11.54	3.56**
9.	Family Prestige (I).	49.93	9.75	48.65	9.42	0.86
10.	Health (J)	37.49	11.23	35.06	8.82	1.53

* P<.05
** P<.01

Table - 6.51
Comparison of Low Achievers of Arts and Commerce Streams on Values

		Low Achievers (Arts) N=81		Low Achievers (Comm.)N=81		
Sl.	Values	M	SD	M	SD	t-value
1.	Religious (A)	45.06	9.53	44.93	12.56	0.10
2.	Social (B)	27.92	9.21	25.27	8.24	1.93
3.	Democratic (C)	37.69	6.74	37.92	8.30	0.19
4.	Aesthetic (D)	54.29	10.90	53.54	15.28	0.36
5.	Economic (E)	48.44	15.41	60.06	8.47	5.95**
6.	Knowledge (F)	41.09	9.18	40.53	12.84	0.32
7.	Hedonistic (G)	65.14	6.99	62.34	9.14	2.20*
8.	Power (H)	63.48	10.45	67.70	11.54	2.44*
9.	Family Prestige (I)	51.23	7.10	48.65	9.42	2.00*
10.	Health (J)	33.01	8.39	35.06	8.82	1.51

* P<.05
** P<.01

Table - 6.52
Comparison of High and Low Achievers of Science Streams on Values

		High Achievers (Science) N=81		Low Achievers (Science) N=81		
Sl.	Values	M	SD	M	SD	t-value
1.	Religious (A)	46.60	9.76	43.33	10.63	2.66**
2.	Social (B)	25.71	9.35	25.53	11.57	0.11
3.	Democratic (C)	37.38	11.78	35.54	6.46	1.23
4.	Acsthetic (D)	53.46	10.86	55.09	7.29	1.12
5.	Economic (E)	57.55	10.19	51.60	15.88	2.84**
6.	Knowledge (F)	37.80	9.56	41.67	10.41	2.46*
7.	Hedonistic (G)	63.67	8.89	61.46	10.70	1.43
8.	Power (H)	64.95	9.24	61.41	10.95	2.22*
9.	Family Prestige (I)	49.90	7.30	49.93	9.75	0.39
10.	Health (J)	35.83	7.09	37.49	11.23	1.12

* P<.05
** P<.01

In pursuance of the objective in chapter 4 of study to compare the values of high and low achievers, significance of difference between relevant means were tested by employing 't'- tests. The obtained results have been presented below in order to test the concerned hypothesis.

The results of analysis with regard to significance of difference in means of students' personal values for high and low achievers together with various subgroups are presented in Tables 6.45 through 6.60.

Table 6.45 shows results pertaining to significance of difference between means of high and low achievers on values. It may be noted that the high achievers yielded significantly higher values on hedonistic and power scale, while the low achievers indicated significantly higher values on social and knowledge scales. In the social, hedonistic and power values the differences between the two groups were found to be significant at .01 level of confidence while knowledge values could attain significance only at .05 level of significance. However the two groups did not differ significantly with respect to six values namely religious, democratic, aesthetic, economic, family prestige and health. Hence the research hypothesis, in chapter 4 namely "there will be significant difference in the values of high and low achievers" was retained with regard to foregoing four values, (*i.e.* social, knowledge, hedonistic and power) and was rejected with regard to foregoing six values (*i.e.* religious, democratic, aesthetic, economic, family prestige and health).

Table 6.46 indicates that high achievers of science and arts streams differed significantly only in three values, namely social ($t=2.38$, $P<.05$), hedonistic ($t=2.39$, $P<.05$) and power ($t=2.61$, $P<.05$). The hypothesis 4.4.5 (b) was accepted at .05 level of confidence. It may be noted that the high achievers of arts stream yielded significantly higher values on hedonistic and power scales, while the high achievers of science stream indicated significantly higher value on social scale. However, the two groups did not differ significantly with respect to seven values, namely religious, democratic, aesthetic, knowledge, family prestige and health values. Hence the research hypothesis in chapter 4 was rejected in case of foregoing seven values.

From Table 6.47 it may be seen that the 't'- values for social, aesthetic and economic values were reported to be significant at .01 level of confidence while hedonistic values could attain significance only at .05 level of confidence. The hypothesis in chapter 4 was accepted. Further, it may be noted that the high achievers of commerce

Table - 6.53
Comparison of High and Low Achievers of Arts Streams on Values

		High Achievers (Arts) N=81		Low Achievers (Arts)N=81		
Sl.	Values	M	SD	M	SD	t-value
1.	Religious (A)	45.06	6.51	45.06	9.53	.00
2.	Social (B)	22.28	8.97	27.92	9.21	3.95**
3.	Democratic (C)	40.17	8.32	37.69	6.74	2.08*
4.	Aesthetic (D)	52.01	10.35	54.29	10.90	1.36
5.	Economic (E)	60.62	12.30	48.44	15.41	5.56**
6.	Knowledge (F)	40.35	8.90	41.09	9.18	1.09
7.	Hedonistic (G)	67.12	9.47	65.14	6.99	1.51
8.	Power (H)	68.50	8.01	63.48	10.45	3.43**
9.	Family Prestige (I)	51.33	8.08	51.23	7.10	0.08
10.	Health (J)	36.00	7.08	33.01	8.39	2.45*

* P<.05
** P<.01

Table - 6.54
Comparison of High and Low Achievers of Commerce Streams on Values

		High Achievers (Comm.) N=81		Low Achievers (Comm.)N=81		
Sl.	Values	M	SD	M	SD	t-value
1.	Religious (A)	45.01	11.34	44.93	12.56	0.04
2.	Social (B)	19.88	10.84	25.27	8.24	3.56**
3.	Democratic (C)	37.48	9.32	37.92	8.30	0.32
4.	Aesthetic (D)	58.32	8.35	53.54	15.28	2.47*
5.	Economic (E)	62.20	8.73	60.06	8.47	1.58
6.	Knowledge (F)	39.39	11.34	40.53	12.84	0.60
7.	Hedonistic (G)	67.65	12.72	62.34	9.14	3.12**
8.	Power (H)	66.81	11.38	67.70	11.54	0.49
9.	Family Prestige (I)	49.83	10.35	48.65	9.42	0.77
10.	Health (J)	35.35	8.54	35.06	8.82	0.21

* P<.05
** P<.01

Table - 6.55
Comparison of High Achievers of Science Stream and Low Achievers of Arts Streams on Values

		High Achievers (Science) N=81		Low Achievers (Arts) N=81		
Sl.	Values	M	SD	M	SD	t-value
1.	Religious (A)	46.60	9.76	45.06	9.53	1.02
2.	Social (B)	25.71	9.35	27.92	9.21	1.40
3.	Democratic (C)	37.38	11.78	37.69	6.74	0.2
4.	Aesthetic (D)	53.46	10.86	54.29	10.90	0.48
5.	Economic (E)	57.55	10.19	48.44	15.41	4.44**
6.	Knowledge (F)	37.80	9.56	41.09	9.18	2.23*
7.	Hedonistic (G)	63.67	8.89	65.14	6.99	1.7
8.	Power (H)	64.95	9.24	63.48	10.45	1.39
9.	Family Prestige (I)	49.90	7.30	51.23	7.10	1.62
10.	Health (J)	35.83	7.09	33.01	8.39	2.31*

* P<.05
** p<.01

Table - 6.56
Comparison of High Achievers of Science Stream and Low Achievers of Commerce Streams on Values

		High Achievers (Science) N=81		Low Achievers (Comm.)N=81		
Sl.	Values	M	SD	M	SD	t-value
1.	Religious (A)	46.60	9.76	44.93	12.56	0.94
2.	Social (B)	25.71	9.35	25.27	8.24	0.32
3.	Democratic (C)	37.38	11.78	37.92	8.30	0.34
4.	Aesthetic (D)	53.46	10.86	53.54	15.28	0.04
5.	Economic (E)	57.55	10.19	60.06	8.47	1.70
6.	Knowledge (F)	37.80	9.56	40.53	12.84	1.53
7.	Hedonistic (G)	63.67	8.89	62.34	9.14	0.94
8.	Power (H)	64.95	9.24	67.70	11.54	1.67
9.	Family Prestige (I)	49.90	7.30	48.65	9.42	0.59
10.	Health (J)	35.83	7.09	35.06	8.82	0.61

NS = Not Significant

Table-6.57

Comparison of High Achievers of Arts Stream and Low Achievers of Science Streams on Values

		High Achievers (Arts) N=81		Low Achievers (Sci.) N=81		
Sl.	Values	M	SD	M	SD	t-value
1.	Religious (A)	45.06	6.51	42.33	10.63	1.97
2.	Social (B)	22.28	8.97	25.53	11.57	1.20
3.	Democratic (C)	40.17	8.32	35.54	6.46	3.96**
4.	Aesthetic (D)	52.01	10.35	55.09	7.29	2.19*
5.	Economic (E)	60.62	12.30	51.60	15.88	4.07**
6.	Knowledge (F)	40.35	8.90	41.67	10.41	0.87
7.	Hedonistic (G)	67.12	9.47	61.46	10.70	3.56**
8.	Power (H)	68.50	8.01	61.41	10.95	4.69**
9.	Family Prestige (I)	51.33	8.08	49.93	9.75	0.99
10.	Health (J)	36.00	7.08	37.49	11.23	1.01

* P<.05
* P<.01

Table - 6.58

Comparison of High Achievers of Arts Stream and Low Achievers of Commerce Streams on Values

		High Achievers (Science) N=81		Low Achievers (Comm.)N=81		
Sl.	Values	M	SD	M	SD	t-value
1.	Religious (A)	45.06	6.51	44.93	12.56	0.08
2.	Social (B)	22.28	8.97	25.27	8.24	2.21*
3.	Democratic (C)	40.17	8.32	37.92	8.30	1.72
4.	Aesthetic (D)	52.01	10.35	53.54	15.28	0.75
5.	Economic (E)	60.62	12.30	60.06	8.47	0.34
6.	Knowledge (F)	40.35	8.90	40.53	12.84	0.10
7.	Hedonistic (G)	67.12	9.47	62.34	9.14	3.27**
8.	Power (H)	68.50	8.01	67.70	11.54	0.51
9.	Family Prestige (I)	51.33	8.08	48.65	9.42	1.94
10.	Health (J)	36.00	7.08	35.06	8.82	0.84

* P<.05
** P<.01

stream scored significantly high on aesthetic, economic and hedonistic values while the high achievers of science stream yielded significantly higher score on social values. On rest of the values, high achievers of science and commerce streams were found to be alike. Hence the hypothesis in chapter 4 was rejected.

It may be seen from Table 6.48 that only one 't'-value (*i.e.* aesthetic, t=4.27, P<.01) was significant at .01 level of confidence. This suggests that the two groups differed significantly with respect to their asethetic values. Hence, the hypothesis in chapter 4 was retained here. Further, greater mean value (58.32) was in favour of high achievers of commerce stream, which implies that high achievers of commerce stream had significantly higher aesthetic values than the high achievers of arts stream. Both the groups, however occupied the similar position in case of rest of the values. Hence research hypothesis in chapter 4 was rejected here.

Table 6.49 demonstrates the results of the application of 't'- test for the differences obtained by low achievers of science and arts streams. It may by noted that the low achievers of arts stream yielded significantly higher values on democratic and hedonistic scales, while the low achievers of science stream indicated significantly higher value on health scale. In all these three values the differences between the two groups were found to be significant.

The two groups did not differ significantly in religious, social, aesthetic, economic, knowledge, power and family prestige values. Hence, the hypothesis in chapter 4 was partly accepted and partly rejected.

Table 6.50 reveals that significant differences existed in means of democratic, economic, and power values as the obtained 't'- values (*i.e.* democratic, t= 2.04, P<.05; economic,t=4.23, P<.01; and power, t=3.56, P<.01) were significant. It may be seen that low achievers of commerce stream appeared to have greater magnitude of democratic, economic and power values in comparison to low achievers of science stream. On rest of the values these two groups were found to be alike. Hence the research hypothesis in chapter 4 was partly retained and partly rejected.

Table 6.51 shows that the low achievers of arts and commerce streams differed significantly with respect to four values, namely economic, hedonistic, power and family prestige. Hence the research hypothesis in chapter 4 was accepted in case of four values. Further the low achievers of arts stream showed superiority over low achievers of commerce stream with reference to hedonistic and family prestige values. On the other hand, low achievers of commerce stream exhibited superiority over low achievers of arts stream with regard to economic and power values. However, both the groups occupied the similar position on rest of the six values and therefore the hypothesis was rejected here.

Significant differences in the value preferences between the high and low achievers of science stream were noted in religious, economic, knowledge and power values (vide Table 6.52). Both the groups differed significantly in respect of those four values. Hence the hypothesis of significant difference in the values of high and low achievers of science stream in chapter 4 was accepted here. In terms of means the high achievers of science stream scored significantly higher on religious, economic and power values. On the other hand, the low achievers of science stream yielded significantly higher on knowledge values. But the two groups did not differ significantly in the rest of the values for which the hypothesis in chapter 4 was rejected.

Table 6.53 exhibits that the high and low achievers of arts stream differed significantly with respect to five values, namely social, democratic, economic, power and health values. Further, the high achievers showed superiority over the low achievers with reference to democratic, economic, power and health values. On the other hand, the low achievers exhibited superiority over the high achievers with regard to social values. Both the groups, however, were found to be similar with regard to religious, aesthetic, knowledge, hedonistic and family prestige values. Hence the hypothesis in chapter 4 was partly retained and partly rejected.

It is evident from Table 6.54 that the high and low achievers of commerce stream differed significantly with respect to social, aesthetic and hedonistic values. It may be noted that the high achievers of commerce stream were significantly more inclined towards aesthetic and hedonistic values, while the low achievers of commerce stream were towards social values. Both the groups, however, did not differ significantly with respect to religious, democratic, economic, knowledge, power, family prestige and health values. In view of the mixed results, the hypothesis in chapter 4 was partly accepted and partly rejected.

Table 6.55 demonstrates that significant differences existed in means of economic, knowledge and health values. It may be observed that the high achievers of science stream appeared to have greater magnitude of economic and health values. while the low achievers of arts stream appeared to have greater magnitude of knowledge values.

Table - 6.59
Comparison of High Achievers of Commerce Stream and Low Achievers of Science Streams on Values

		High Achievers (Comm.) N=81		Low Achievers (Sci.) N=81		
Sl.	Values	M	SD	M	SD	t-value
1.	Religious (A)	45.01	11.34	42.33	10.63	1.55
2.	Social (B)	19.88	10.84	25.53	11.57	3.21**
3.	Democratic (C)	37.48	9.32	35.54	6.46	1.54
4.	Aesthetic (D)	58.32	8.35	55.09	7.29	2.62*
5.	Economic (E)	62.20	8.73	51.60	15.88	5.26**
6.	Knowledge (F)	39.39	11.34	41.67	10.41	1.33
7.	Hedonistic (G)	67.65	12.72	61.46	10.70	3.35**
8.	Power (H)	66.81	11.38	61.41	10.95	3.07**
9.	Family Prestige (I)	49.83	10.35	49.93	9.75	0.06
10.	Health (J)	35.35	8.54	37.49	11.23	1.36

* P<.05
** P<.01

Table - 6.60
Comparison of High Achievers of Commerce Stream and Low Achievers of Arts Streams on Values

		High Achievers (Comm.) N=81		Low Achievers (Arts) N=81		
Sl.	Values	M	SD	M	SD	t-value
1.	Religious (A)	45.01	11.34	45.06	9.53	.03
2.	Social (B)	19.88	10.84	27.92	9.21	5.08**
3.	Democratic (C)	37.48	9.32	37.69	6.74	0.16
4.	Aesthetic (D)	58.32	8.35	54.29	10.90	2.54*
5.	Economic (E)	62.20	8.73	48.44	15.41	6.99**
6.	Knowledge (F)	39.39	11.34	41.09	9.18	1.05
7.	Hedonistic (G)	67.65	12.72	65.14	6.99	1.56
8.	Power (H)	66.81	11.38	63.48	10.45	1.94
9.	Family Prestige (I)	49.83	10.35	51.23	7.10	1.01
10.	Health (J)	35.35	8.54	33.01	8.39	1.76

* P<.05
** P<.01

On rest of the values, high achievers of science stream and low achievers of arts stream were found to be alike. Hence the research hypothesis in chapter 4 was partly accepted and partly rejected.

It can be seen from Table 6.56 that none of the 't'-values computed between the high achievers of science stream and low achievers of commerce stream turned out to be significant. Therefore, these two groups did not differ significantly in any of the values. Hence, the hypothesis of significant difference between the high achievers of science stream and the low achievers of commerce stream on values in chapter 4 was rejected.

A close examination of Table 6.57 indicates that the obtained 't'-values for democratic, aesthetic, economic, hedonistic and power values were found to be significant, hence the research hypothesis in chapter 4 was retained. This observation leads to the inference that the high achievers of arts stream and low achievers of science stream differed significantly with each other in their democratic, aesthetic, economic, hedonistic and power values. It may be noted that the high achievers of arts stream scored significantly higher on democratic, economic, hedonistic and power, values while, the low achievers of science stream yielded significantly higher values on aesthetic scale. The two groups, however, did not differ significantly in religious, social, knowledge, family prestige, and health values. Hence the hypothesis in chapter 4 was rejected here.

A close perusal of Table 6.58 revealed significance of two 't'-values, one for social values ($t=2.21$, $P<.05$) and the other for hedonistic ($t=3.27$, $P<.01$) which suggest significant differences in social and hedonistic values between these two groups. It may be observed that the high achievers of arts stream yielded significantly higher values on hedonistic scale, while the low achievers of commerce stream indicated significantly higher values on social scale. The two groups, however, did not differ significantly with respect to religious, democratic, aesthetic, economic, knowledge, power, family prestige and health. Hence the hypothesis in chapter 4 was partly accepted and partly rejected.

Table 6.59 exhibits that the high achievers of commerce stream and the low achievers of science stream differed significantly with respect to five values namely social, aesthetic, economic, hedonistic and power. Hence the hypothesis in chapter 4 was accepted in case of those five values. Further, the high achievers of commerce stream shows superiority over low achievers of science stream with reference to aesthetic, economic, hedonistic and power values. On the other hand, the low achievers of science stream exhibited superiority over the high achievers of commerce stream with regard to social values. On rest of the values, these two groups were found to be alike. Hence the hypothesis in chapter 4 was rejected here.

A close scrutiny of Table 6.60 would reveal that the obtained 't' values for social, aesthetic and economic values were found to be significant. Hence the research hypothesis in chapter 4 was retained. This observation leads to the inference that the high achievers of commerce stream and the low achievers of arts stream differed significantly with each other in their social, aesthetic and economic values. It may be noted that the high achievers of commerce stream scored significantly higher on aesthetic and economic values, while the low achievers of arts stream indicated higher values on social scale. however, no significant differences between the two groups were noticed on religious, democratic, knowledge, hedonistic, power, family prestige and health values. Hence the hypothesis in chapter 4 was rejected here.

7
SUMMARY AND CONCLUSIONS

INTRODUCTION

Human beings of the present era are enthralled with the advancement of Science as well as encountering the several complexities which are the ultimate by-products of any scientific progression. There is concern for behavioural stability amidst the changing social systems. The need for behavioural re-orientation to match the current trends of the world is also felt. Mankind has been constantly striving for emancipation, *i.e.* freedom to choose its own destiny. During its long and chequered history, mankind has developed three forces to control its group destiny *viz.* Social, political and economic, and evolved some sort of value system to provide life and blood to the individual and society. Every known society has a value system—a set of rules and goals that guide its conduct and the judgements. The business of social life proceeds on the assumption that the values established in the groups are the ones that must be respected and enforced. With this end in view, every cultured society has developed some educational system to operate within its socio-economic and political system because education is one of the potent factors most likely to influence and modify one's behaviour. The social scientists (Rokeach, 1973, Schiffman and Kanuk, 1983; and Korpar *et al.* 1986) have kept their faith on 'value' approach either to induce change in behaviour or to gauge the stable value system in the individual's personality framework.

From the above discussion, it is apparent that the search for a sound philosophy that can sustain the human race in this 'nuclear age' is but 'Spirituality' and this spirituality is what is missing today, with all the advances in science and technology, there is more conflict and greater misery because spirituality was missing. Further the downward pull of the forces like freedom, adventure, creative imagination, clarity of thinking had sealed the fact of many civilisations, in the past and it is threatening to destroy our intellectual and moral fibre today. But fortunately the light of the mind has not been totally put out all over the world and history is replete with instances of how the mind has devised its own ways of eventually overpowering its captors. Even when harshly harassed for giving expression to their unpopular views or ideas, men of the calibre of socrates, Christ, Lincoln, Gandhiji and Radhakrishnan courageously upheld their convictions and the right of man to freedom of thought. Galileo was pressured to give up his support to the Copernician theory under threat of torture. But even as he was signing the recantation, he is said to have muttered. Thus the great martyrs of history have been those who undauntedly perceived the truth whether in the realm of knowledge of values and who were ready, when necessary, to make the supreme sacrifice.

The quality of life, therefore, cannot be enhanced without the unhampered pilgrimage of the mind towards truth and excellence which constitute the power of house of creativity and the spring-board for all human values, our educational institutions will have to stress the significance of thought and moral values because, as the late prof. Saiyidain (1962) tellingly remarks "without the saving grace of free end swift thought, man would be reduced to the level of a mere pygmy, a speck of dust dancing helplessly in the wind for a brief meaningless second, on one of the smallest of the innumerable planets". Higher creative life is the clearest and purest expression of the essential characteristic of life a all its points and levels. All life, however commonplace, is saturated with the self-same elements whose inflore scence is literature, philosophy, science, art and religion. They proclaim the victory of the creative human spirit striving towards more truth, more goodness, more beauty and more light. But modern education that different educational institutions are expected to impart, has to address itself to the lofty tasks of emancipating man's mind from the stranglehold of conservatism and obscurantism. Vivekananda (1932) condemns man's reactionary tendency to seek asylum in the moth-eaten traditions of his forefathers and invest them with an unjustified sanctity. Man's true life as Russell (1940) has aptly argued, consists not in the satisfaction of his pressing physical wants but "in art and thought and love in the creation and contemplation of beauty and in the scientific understanding of the world".

The greatest need of today is that man in his mad race in pursuit of transient materialistic gains and objectives, should at least occasionally, pause and reflect on the real purpose and value of human life and give a fresh orientation to his view of his life based on such introspective reflection. If this were done one should have no difficulty to realise that amongst all living species the human being occupies a special and exalted place by reason fo his alone being endowed with powers of reason and discrimination aided by a discerning intellect and faculties of analytical thinking, assimilation and recollection. From time immemorial these special gifts have generated in man in keen sense of inquiry in search of truth, wisdom and bliss.

The most precious asset possessed by our country is our glorious ancient culture firmly founded on the principles of 'Sanathan Dharma'. This culture has been handed down form generation to generation during the past thousands of years and it lies enbedded in the hearts and souls of the millions of our people belonging to different religious faiths who are knit together by this common cultural bond. Unless the training given to our children is such as to acquaint them with the fundamentals of the glorious ancient culture of India and develop in their minds a deep and abiding respect for all faiths as well as a keen sense of pride about our unique cultural heritage, the preservation of our cultural heritage will be seriously imperilled.

Of all the countries in the world, we in India have the richest cultural and spiritual heritage. But values in the modern world are changing so rapidly that the young find themselves quite bewildered when they try to form their value perspectives or when they try to cherish or choose values. "The rate of change", as Gajjar (1985) writes, "in the context of value is increasing so fast as to cause a shock". Raths *et al.* (1966) express the predicaments of the students in the following words.

"It seems to us that the pace and complexity of modern life has so exacerbated the problem of deciding what is good and what is right and what is desirable that large number of children are finding it increasingly bewildering, even overwhelming, to decide what is worth valuing, what is worth time an energy"

In India the whole population in general and the students in particular, due to their inexperience are facing the same problems, because, as Thomas (1970) puts it, "the traditional values are weakened and new values are emerging". In this context the Indian Education commission (1964-66) points out.

"The old values, which held society together are disappearing and as there is no effective programme to replace them by a new sense of social responsibility, innumerable signs of social disorganisation are evident everywhere and are continually on the increase. These include strikes, increasing lawlessness, and a disregard for public property, corruption in public life and communal tensions and troubles. Student unrest of which so much is written, is only one and is probably a minor one of these symptoms".

Thus there is the need of a comprehensive programme of value education which can enable students to meet new situations in the world of values, not only as they are now, but also in any new situation that may arise in future.

Mental health which is so badly lacking among many in the modern world, one comes to know, as Gajjar (1985) does on the basis of studies, that "besides physiological, biochemical, social, cultural and human relationship factors affective experiences and other needs and purposes of the individuals inner life are of importance". This necessitates a programme of value education which make the students aware of their inner lives, and train them how to synthesize the needs and purpose of the inner lives with those of the outer.

The time has come to act. The call now is, Do ! leap into the branch and save the world. All this rests on our educational institutions to harness the inner potentials of their students and channelise them in such a way that their intellectual pursuits promote and strengthen appropriate attitudes, respect of the diversity cultures and the dignity and freedom of the individual and adopt traditional values to the new conditions and needs that are evolving.

It is clear from the above discussion that value system plays an important role in the decision making process. In fact every human action is the reflection of personal or social values. The present situation of India calls for a system of education which apart from strengthening national unity must strengthen social solidarity through meaningful and constructive value education. Before launching any comprehensive educational programme to promote students' personal values, it is essential to study the prevalent value systems held by the students.

Thus, the present study is an humble attempt in that direction.

ASSUMPTIONS

(i) The values of students is a significant area of study, although neglected so far in educational research.

(ii) Values of students are quantifiable and happen to be a function of several psychological factors of which academic achievement is one of them.

(iii) Having studied the factors, mainly the achievement, associated with values of students, steps could be taken up to enhance it so that the deterioration of values be checked.

(iv) Students with positive values are the assets of the society.

OBJECTIVES OF THE STUDY

(i) To determine the value profile of the higher secondary students across their academic stream (*i.e.* Science, Arts and Commerce), residential background (*i.e.* rural and urban), sex (Male and Female) and achievement level (*i.e.* high achievers and low achievers).

(ii) To compare the value patterns of higher secondary students belonging to different academic streams (*i.e.* Science, Arts and Commerce).

(iii) To compare the values of higher secondary rural and urban students across their academic streams.

(iv) To compare the values of higher secondary male and female students across their academic streams.

(v) To compare the values of high and low achievers at the higher secondary level of education across their academic streams.

HYPOTHESES

(i) The higher secondary students will have differential value profiles in terms of their academic stream, residential background, sex and achievement level.

(ii) Value patterns of students as represented by three different academic streams (*i.e.* Science, Arts and Commerce) of higher Secondary education will be significantly different.

(iii) There will be significant difference in the values of :

(a) Rural and Urban students.
(b) Arts rural and Science rural students.
(c) Science rural and Commerce rural students.
(d) Arts rural and Commerce rural students.
(e) Arts urban and Science urban students.
(f) Science urban and Commerce urban students.
(g) Arts urban and Commerce urban students.
(h) Science urban and Science rural students.
(i) Arts urban and Arts rural students.
(j) Commerce urban and Commerce rural students.
(k) Science urban and Arts rural students.
(l) Science urban and Commerce rural students.
(m) Arts urban and Science rural students.
(n) Arts urban and Commerce rural students.
(o) Commerce urban and Science rural students.
(p) Commerce urban and Arts rural students.

(iv) There will be significant difference in the values of :

(a) Male and Female students.
(b) Arts male and Science male students.
(c) Science male and Commerce male students.
(d) Arts male and Commerce male students.
(e) Arts female and Science female students.
(f) Science female and Commerce female students.
(g) Arts female and Commerce female students.
(h) Science male and Science female students.
(i) Arts male and Arts female students.
(j) Commerce male and Commerce female students.
(k) Science male and Arts female students.
(l) Science male and Commerce female students.
(m) Arts male and Science female students.
(n) Arts male and Commerce female students.
(o) Commerce male and Science female students.
(p) Commerce male and Arts female students.

(v) There will be significant difference in the values of :

(a) High Achievers and Low Achievers.
(b) High Achievers of Science and Arts streams.
(c) High Achievers of Science and Commerce streams.
(d) High Achievers of Arts and Commerce streams.
(e) Low Achievers of Science stream and Low Achievers of Arts stream.
(f) Low Achievers of Science stream and Low Achievers of Commerce stream.
(g) Low Achievers of Arts stream and Low Achievers of Commerce stream.
(h) High and Low Achievers of Science stream.
(i) High and Low Achievers of Arts stream.
(j) High and Low Achievers of Commerce stream.
(k) High Achievers of Science stream and Low Achievers of Arts stream.
(l) High Achievers of Science stream and Low Achievers of Commerce stream.
(m) High Achievers of Arts stream and Low Achievers of Science stream.
(n) High Achievers of Arts stream and Low Achievers of Commerce stream.

(o) High Achievers of Commerce stream and Low Achievers of Science stream.

(p) High Achievers of Commerce stream and Low Achievers of Arts stream.

METHOD OF THE STUDY

So far as the research methodology is concerned, the present study comes under the scope of "Descriptive Research", this is a status study of descriptive nature made on the basis of data gathered through field investigation. So the method to be more exact, followed in this investigation was said to be the "Descriptive Survey", under "casual-comparative" one.

SAMPLE

The data were collected from twelve institutions, both government and private aided institutions. These institutions were randomly drawn with the help of lottery method. It was primarily decided to take up at least 900 subjects of +2 stage (*i.e.* final year), spreaded over three academic streams (*i.e.* Science, Arts and Commerce) for final analysis of the study. Thus from each academic streams a sample of 300 students was drawn randomly. In order to compare the high and low achievers with respect to their values, a sample of 243 high achievers (*i.e.* 81 from each academic stream, based on Kelly's dichotomy) and 243 low achievers (*i.e.* following the same procedure) was drawn.

TOOLS USED

Students' values was measured by the personal values Questionnaire (PVQ) which has been developed by Sherry and Verma (1978). No specific test was used to obtain data on student's achievement. The average of the marks in the annual examination of class XI and the half-yearly examination of class XII were used for the purpose.

COLLECTION OF DATA

The selected students were administered the PVQ in the classes of their respective institutions. Necessary report was established through personal contacts. The purpose of the study was explained to them. The respondents were requested to answer the questions sincerely and frankly. They were assured that the responses would be kept strictly confidential. Necessary instructions were given to them before the administration of the test.

DATA TREATMENT

The main purpose of this study was to compare the values of students belonging to different academic streams. The data obtained on values for each stream (N=300) were tabulated separately into frequency distributions. Mean scores and SDs of each group on values were calculated. Profiles for different groups were prepared on the basis of mean scores and plotted in figures to give a comparative picture. The comparison between different groups was made on the basis of the 't'-test.

MAJOR FINDINGS

The preceding chapter has been devoted to the analysis and interpretation of data. The analysis has yielded some significant findings. Such findings relate to (i) values of students—the profile analysis, (ii) comparison fo student's personal values across their academic streams, (iii) comparison of values of rural and urban students, (iv) comparison of values of male and female students, and (v) comparison of values of high and low achievers. Therefore, the major findings have been presented under those heads:

Values of Students : The Profile Analysis

○ ***Study of Value profiles Across the Academic Streams***

- The higher secondary students belonging to science, arts and commerce streams had their own unique value profiles.
- The value profile encompassed the highest preference for power values among arts and commerce students along with its matched least preference for social values.
- The science students ranked highest to hedonistic values and lowest to social values.
- Similarity regarding the preference of values, namely economic, (*i.e.* 3rd rank), aesthetic (*i.e.* 4th rank), family prestige (*i.e.* 5th rank), religious (*i.e.* 6th rank), and health (*i.e.* 9th rank) among science, arts and commerce students were observed.
- There were deviations in value profiles in respect to the positions of power, hedonistic, democratic and know-ledge values between the science and arts students, and between the science and commerce students.

○ ***Study of Value Profiles Across the Residential Back-ground***

- The value profile encompassed the highest preference for democratic values among the rural-urban students along with its matched least preference for health values.

- Similarity regarding the preference of values, namely democratic (*i.e.* 1st rank), aesthetic (*i.e.* 3rd rank), and health (*i.e.* 10th rank) in both the groups of students (*i.e.* rural vs urban) were observed.
- There were deviations in value profiles in respect to the positions of social, hedonistic, knowledge, economic, religious, family prestige and power values for the rural and urban students.

○ ***Study of Value Profiles Across the Sex***

- The most preferred value for the male students was power values and for the female students was hedonistic values. However, both male and female students preferred least the social values.
- Similarity in ranks of family prestige (5th), religious (6th), knowledge (7th), democratic (8th), health (9th) and social (10th) values was noticed for the male and female students.
- There were deviations in value profiles in respect to the positions of power, hedonistic, aesthetic, and economic values for the male and female students.

○ ***Study of Value Profiles Across the Academic Achievement***

- The value profile encompassed the highest preference for power values among the high and low achievers along with its matched least preference for social values.
- Similarity in ranks of hedonistic (2nd), family prestige (5th), religious (6th), knowledge (7th), democratic (8th) and health (9th) values was observed for the high and low achievers.
- There were deviations in value profiles in respect to the positions of economic and aesthetic values for the high and low achievers.

Comparison of Higher Secondary Students on Values :

○ ***Comparison of Values of Students Belonging to Different Academic Streams***

- The science and arts students differed significantly in social, democratic, hedonistic and power values. The science students had higher democratic and hedonistic values while the arts students had greater magnitude of social and power values.
- Significant differences between the science and commerce students were found with respect to their democratic, economic, knowledge, power and family prestige values. The science students had scored significantly higher values on democratic,

knowledge and family prestige scales, while the commerce students yielded significantly higher values on economic and power scales.

- There were significant differences between the arts and commerce students on social, aesthetic, economic, power and family prestige values. The arts students yielded significantly higher values on social and family prestige scales, while the commerce students indicated higher values on aesthetic, economic and power scales.

Comparison of Rural and Urban Students and Various Sub-Groups on Values :

- As a whole, when total rural and urban students irrespective of their academic streams were compared, it was found that the urban students had scored significantly higher means on all the ten values namely religious, social, democratic, aesthetic, economic, knowledge, hedonistic, power, family prestige and health.
- The rural students belonging to arts and science streams differed significantly in social, democratic, aesthetic, economic, knowledge, power, family prestige and health values. The arts students having rural background yielded significantly higher values on economic and knowledge scales, while the science students having rural background were found to have more social, democratic, aesthetic, power, family prestige and health values.
- When the rural students of science and commerce streams were compared, it was found that there were significant differences on social, democratic, aesthetic, hedonistic, power family prestige and health values. The rural students of science stream yielded significantly higher scores on all these seven values.
- The rural students of arts and commerce streams did not differ significantly with respect to their religious, aesthetic, power, family prestige and health values. However, significant differences were noted on social, democratic, economic, knowledge and hedonistic values. The arts rural students had scored higher mean on social, economic, knowledge and hedonistic values, whereas the commerce rural students scored higher mean on democratic values.
- Striking differences have been observed in the mean values of arts and science students having urban background with regard

to all the ten scales and the differences were in favour of science urban students.

- The science urban students, when compared, to the commerce urban students, it was found that there were significant differences between them with respect to religious, social, democratic, aesthetic, economic, knowledge, family prestige and health values. The science urban students yielded significantly higher scores on social, democratic, aesthetic, economic, knowledge, family prestige and health values. On the other hand, the commerce urban students indicated significantly higher score on religious values.
- On all ten values there were significant differences in the mean scores of arts and commerce students having urban background. The commerce urban students had shown higher mean scores on all the ten values.
- The urban and rural science students differed significantly on all the ten values. The science students having urban background had higher scores on all the ten values.
- There were significant differences between the urban and rural arts students with respect to social, democratic, economic, knowledge, hedonistic, power, family prestige and health values. The arts students having urban background were found to have more democratic, power family prestige and health values while their rural counterparts were having more social, economic, knowledge and hedonistic values.
- With respect to value patterns of urban and rural commerce students the hypothesis was accepted. The commerce students having urban background had shown higher mean scores on all the ten values, namely religious, social, democratic, aesthetic, economic, knowldege, hedonistic, power, family prestige and health than their rural counterparts.
- When the science urban and the arts rural students were compared it was revealed that there were significant mean differences on all the ten values and differences were in favour of the science urban students.
- The science urban students in comparison to the commerce rural students appeared to have greater magnitude of values on all the ten scales.
- The arts students having urban background differed significantly from the science students having rural background in respect to their mean scores on social, democratic, aesthetic, economic,

hedonistic and family prestige values. The science rural students yielded significantly higher values on all these six scales than their arts urban counterparts.

- The arts urban and the commerce rural students differed significantly with respect to eight values, namely religious, economic, hedonistic, power, democratic, aesthetic, family prestige and health. The arts urban students showed superiority over the commerce rural students with reference to religious, democratic, hedonistic, power, family prestige and health values. On the other hand, the commerce rural students exhibited superiority over the arts urban students with regard to aesthetic and economic values.
- Significant differences existed in means of the commerce urban and science rural students with respect to religious, democratic, aesthetic, economic, knowledge, hedonistic, and power values. The commerce urban students appeared to have greater magnitude of religious, aesthetic, economic, knowledge, hedonistic, and power values in comparison to the science rural students. On the other hand, the science rural students yielded significantly higher values on democratic scale.
- Significant differences have been noticed in the means scores of commerce urban and arts rural students with regard to all the ten values and the differences were in favour of commerce urban students.

Comparison of Male and Female Students and Various Sub-Groups on Values :

- As a whole when male and female students (irrespective of their streams) were compared, it was found that the male students had scored significantly higher means on aesthetic, hedonistic, power, family prestige and health values while the female students indicated significantly higher values on social and economic scales.
- In the five values namely religious, aesthetic, economic, knowledge and health the differences between the arts and science male students were found to be significant. The science male students yielded significantly higher values on all the aforesaid scales.
- The science and commerce male students differed significantly in social, hedonistic, power, family prestige and health values. The science male students were significantly more inclined

towards social, family prestige and health values than the commerce male students. On the other hand the commerce male students had significantly higher values on hedonistic and power scales than their science counterparts.

- Significant differences have been observed in the mean scores of arts and commerce male students with respect to social, economic, knowledge, hedonistic, power and family prestige values. The commerce male students appeared to have greater magnitude of economic, knowledge, hedonistic and power values while the arts male students indicated greater magnitude of social and family prestige values.
- The arts and science female students differed significantly with respect to social, democratic, aesthetic, knowldege, hedonistic, power and family prestige values. The arts female students showed superiority over science female students on all those seven values.
- With respect to value pattern of science and commerce female students it was revealed that on aesthetic, economic, hedonistic, power and family prestige values, the commerce female students scored significantly higher mean values than their science female counterparts. While on religious values, mean score obtained by the science female students was significantly higher than the commerce female students.
- The arts and commerce female students differed significantly with respect to religious, social, power and health values. The arts female students showed superiority over commerce female students with respect to religious, social and health values while the commerce female students exhibited superiority over arts female students on power values.
- When the male and female students of science stream were compared, it was found that the science male students were having greater magnitude of aesthetic, hedonistic, power, family prestige and health values. In all these five values the differences between the two groups were found to be significant.
- Significant differences in the value preferences between arts male and female students were noted in social, economic, knowledge, power, family prestige and health scale. In terms of their mean scores arts female students indicated significantly higher values on social, economic, knowledge and health scales, while arts male students yielded significantly higher values on power and family prestige scales.

- There were significant differences in the value patterns of the commerce male and female students with respect to religious, economic, hedonistic, power and health scales. The commerce male students scored significantly high on religious, hedonistic, power and health values while commerce female students demonstrated significantly higher scores on economic values.
- The science male and arts female students differed significantly with each other in their social, democratic, aesthetic, economic, power and family prestige values. The science male students scored significantly high on aesthetic, power and family prestige values, while arts female students exhibited significantly higher scores on social, democratic and economic values.
- The science male and commerce female students differed significantly only in religious, economic, family prestige and health values. The science male students yielded significantly higher values on religious, family prestige and health scales while the commerce female students indicated significantly higher values on economic scale.
- Significant differences have been observed in the mean scores of arts male and science female students with regard to their aesthetic, economic, hedonistic, power and family prestige values. The arts male students scored significantly high on aesthetic, hedonistic, power and family prestige values, while sicence female students demonstrated significantly higher score on economic values.
- The arts male and commerce female students differed significantly only in three values namely economic, power and family prestige. The arts male students yielded significantly higher values on power and family prestige scales, while the commerce female students indicated significantly higher values on economic scale.
- The commerce male and science female students differed significantly with each other in their aesthetic, hedonistic, power and family prestige values. The commerce male students scored significantly higher on all these four values than their science female counterparts.
- Significant differences have been noticed in the mean scores of commerce male and arts female students with regard to social, aesthetic, economic, hedonistic, and power values. The commerce male students exhibited significantly higher values on aesthetic, hedonistic and power scales while the arts female

students yielded significantly higher values on social and economic scales.

Comparison of High and Low Achievers and Various Sub-Groups on Values :

- As a whole, when high and low achievers (irrespective of their streams) were compared, it was found that there were significant differences between the two groups in social, knowledge, hedonistic, and power values. The high achievers yielded significantly higher values on hedonistic and power scales, while the low achievers indicated significantly higher values on social and knowledge scales.
- The high achievers of science and arts streams differed significantly only in three values, namely social, hedonistic and power. The high achievers of arts stream yielded significantly higher values on hedonistic and power scales, while the high achievers of science stream indicated significantly higher values on social scale.
- Significant differences between the high achievers of science and commerce streams were observed with respect to their social, aesthetic, economic and hedonistic values. The high achievers of commerce stream scored significantly high on aesthetic, economic, and hedonistic values while the high achievers of science stream indicated significantly higher value on social scale.
- The high achievers of arts and commerce streams differed significantly in their aesthetic values and the difference goes in favour of high achievers of commerce stream.
- In the three values, namely democratic, hedonistic and health the differences between the low achievers of science and arts streams were reported to be significant. The low achievers of arts stream yielded significantly higher values on democratic and hedonistic scales, while the low achievers of science stream indicated significantly higher value on health scale.
- Only three values namely democratic, economic, and power emerged significant when the low achievers of science and commerce streams were compared and the difference favoured the low achievers of commerce stream.
- The low achievers of arts and commerce streams differed significantly with respect to ecnomic, hedonistic, power and family prestige values. The low achievers of arts stream showed

superiority over low achievers of commerce stream with reference to hedonistic and family prestige values. On the other hand, low achievers of commerce stream exhibited superiority over low achievers of arts stream with regard to economic and power values.

- Significant differences in the value preferences between the high and low achievers of science stream were noted in religious, economic, knowledge and power values. The high achievers of science stream scored significantly higher on religious, economic and power values, while the low achievers of science stream yielded significantly higher on knowledge values.
- The high and low achievers of arts stream differed significantly with respect to social, democratic, economic, power and health values. The high achievers (arts) showed superiority over the low achievers with reference to democratic, economic, power and health values while the low achievers exhibited superiority over the high achievers (arts) in social values.
- Only three values, namely social, aesthetic and hedonistic emerged significant when the high and low achievers of commerce stream were compared. The high achievers of commerce stream were significantly more inclined towards aesthetic and hedonistic values, while low achievers of commerce stream were more inclined towards social values.
- Significant differences existed in means of economic, knowledge and health values between the high achievers of science stream and low achievers of arts stream. The high achievers of science stream appeared to have greater magnitude of economic and health values while the arts low achievers appeared to have greater magnitude of knowledge values.
- No significant variations were found between the high achievers of science stream and low achievers of commerce stream in their value preferences.
- The high achievers of arts stream and low achievers of science stream differed significantly with each other in their democratic, aesthetic, economic, hedonistic, and power values. The high achievers of arts stream scored significantly higher on democratic, economic, hedonistic and power values, whereas the low achievers of science stream yielded significantly higher value on aesthetic scale.
- The high achievers of arts stream differed significantly from the low achievers of commerce stream in social and hedonistic

values. The high achievers of arts stream yielded significantly higher value on hedonistic scale, while the low achievers of commerce stream indicated significantly higher value on social scale.

- The higher achievers of commerce stream and the low achievers of science stream diferred significantly with regard to social, aesthetic, economic, hedonistic and power values. The high achievers of commerce stream showed superiority over low achievers of science stream with reference to aesthetic, economic, hedonistic and power values. On the other hand, the low achievers of science stream exhibited superiority over the high achievers of commerce stream with regard to social values.
- In social, aesthetic and economic values the differences between the high achievers of commerce stream and the low achievers of arts stream were reported to be significant. The high achievers of commerce stream scored significantly higher on aesthetic and economic values while the low achievers of arts stream indicated higher values on social scale.

DISCUSSION

As regards the value profiles of students across their streams, it was found that there were significant resemblances among the students of the three academic streams, namely science, arts and commerce. Both the arts and commerce students placed power values on the top, it reflects that they are more interested in occupying higher position where they can exercise authority and maintain strict discipline having ability to control over their subordinate employees. On the other hand, the prominence of hedonistic values in the science students pinpoints the fact that the science students try to derive satisfaction from physical comfort and rest with the emphasis on fulfilment of personal desires. This has well been echoed in their ranking of social values as the least one. It is quite surprising to note that all the students (irrespective of their stream) have a least preference for social values. This is quite natural for a student who lovers power and fulfilment of personal desires. He never bothers for kindness, sympathy and for the general walfare of the community. Social values carry less weight for him. The obtained results of the presents study with regard to the value profile of students across their academic stream are contradictory to the findings of Das (1983) who found that religious values and aesthetic values were the most preferred and least preferred values respectively for the arts students. Power and family prestige values were equally most preferred values for the science students alongwith aesthetic values as the least one. The most preferred value for the commerce students was economic values and the least one was democratic values.

It was further found that the value profile encompassed the highest preference for democratic values among the rural-urban students along with its matched least preference for health values. The obtained findings do not get support from any study because nobody has studied value profile of rural and urban students. The preference for democratic values in both the rural and urban students hints that they are more interested in ensuring equal rights to all and trying to maintain impartiality among race, class or religion. They believe in taking their own choices or decisions and respecting all regardless of rich and poor. Their fundamental belief is that there should not be any discrimination among persons on the basis of caste, colour, religion and language. Further their least perference for health values indicate that they are less conscious of their food habits, effect of physical exercise for maintenance of health and the consequences of bad health.

Another finding indicates that the most preferred value for the male students was power values and for females hedonistic values. It implies that the male students are more oriented towards exercise of their authority and to maintain strict discipline so as to have control over their subordinate employees. On the other hand, the female students are more pleasure seekers and try to avoid pains. They derive satisfaction from physical comfort and rest. They believe in the fulfilment of personal desires. However, both the male and female students preferred least the social values. It is but natural that those who are oriented towards exercise of the authority and to have control over their subordinate employees together with fulfilment of personal desires will have less concern for the group welfare. They justify their authority without sympathy and kindness. Social values do not appeal to them. The obtained results of the present study with regard to the value profile of students across their sex are contradictory to the findings of Dwivedi (1983), Patni (1983), Mishra (1991), Das (1993), Nayak (1994) and Singh (1997) who reported different value profiles of male and female students.

It was further observed that the value profile encompassed the highest preference for power values among the high and low achievers along with its matched least preference for social values. The prominence of power values in the high and low achievers points out that both of them are more interested in occupying higher position where they can exercise power and can control their subordinate employees. Their least preference for social values indicate that they are least concerned with the general walfare of the community. They do not bother for kindness and sympathy. Thus social values carry less weight for them. There are no empirical evidences available which render direct support to the findings of the present study. However, the study of Rath (1994), employing different tool of value, has shown that values possessed in the dimension of personal, educational, and materialistic of high achievers were more than the low achievers while values possessed by low achievers in the areas of religious, socialistic and humanistic were more than the high achievers.

Another finding of the study highlights the superiority of science students over the arts students with regard to democratic and hedonistic values. This leads to the conclusion that the students of science stream like to maintain impartiality among different races, classes and religions and thus ensure equal rights to all. They like to respect every body without any discrimination. They believe in exercising one's own choices or talking decisions in different walks of life. The objective analysis of life might have prompted them to ascribe more liking for democratic values. Further the science students have attached more liking to hedonistic values. This suggests that science students try to derive satisfaction from physical comfort and rest with the emphasis on fulfilment of personal desires. This finding can not be rationalized because generally science students are more painstaker and hardworker.

On the other hand, arts students have inclination towards social and power values. It implies that arts students are concerned with the general welfare of the community by occupying higher position and power. In other words, it can be said that in order to serve the society one needs to occupy some position.

It was also found that science students have more preference for the democratic, knowledge and family prestige values than the commerce students. It implies that science students respect the individuality of others and disfavour any kind of discrimination on the grounds of caste, creed, colour, religion etc. Further they have much interest in theoretical principles of any activity. They have love for discovery of truth and belief in hard work. They prefer to study for advancement of knowledge. Besides, they are quite aware of the prestige of own family. They do not like to work which will degrade their family prestige.

On the other hand, commerce students have inclination towards economic and power values. This may be attributed to the nature of the educational course itself. The whole network of the courses revolved mostly around the topics like economic conditions and considerations as well as monetary transcations which resulted in such an economic outlook. Economic sufficiency does not bring only physical comforts but also the power. For the commerce students economic sufficiency can be attained by occupying some position.

The arts students have shown higher preference for social and family prestige values than the commerce students. This leads to the conclusion that arts students like to render social services and work for the general welfare of the community. They are kind and sympathetic and trouble none. They have also concern for their family prestige. They do not like to do anything which will defame or degrade their family prestige.

On the other hand, commerce students have more liking for aesthetic, economic and power values. The preference of commerce students for economic and power values has also been observed when they were compared to science students. It may be discussed in the same light. But it is quite interesting to note that in the midst of power and pecuniary gain, the commerce students have shown their appreciation for finer aspects of creative life. The obtained results of the present study with regard to academic stream differences in values of students are contradictory to the findings of Das (1993) who found significant differences in some values of students belonging to different academic streams. Patni (1983) has also reported the faculty differences in values but his findings are not in consonance with the results of the present one.

The overall findings with regard to rural-urban differences highlight the superiority of urban students over the rural students with respect to all the ten values. These results hinted that urban environment is more conducive for the development of values. It is a general notion that the urban enviornment which contaminated the minds of the youths through ill effects of rampant industrialization, urbanization and modernization was shattered. However, these findings need further investigation. Some studies, employing the present tool or different tools of values have shown differences in values of rural and urban students (Gaur, 1975; Zamen, 1982; Dwivedi, 1983; Verma, Das and Swain 1993; and Nayak, 1994). But the findings of these researches are not in consonance with the results of the present one.

The overall findings with regard to male-female differences indicate the superiority of male students over the female students with regard to aesthetic, hedonistic, power, family prestige and health values. It is interesting to note that in the midst of lust for pleasure, power and prestige of the family, the male students have shown their appreciation for finer aspects of creative life and health. On the other hand, female students have shown their inclination towards social and economic values. This leads to the conclusion that female students like to do social service, think for social welfare, enjoy friendship, help needy persons and think for the development of the community. In addition, they like to be economically self-sufficient. They want to take up jobs which would give them opportunity to make a lot of money and thus stand on their own legs. For them education should be imparted to enable earning for livelihood. In several studies male and female students have exhibited significant differences in values (De and Jaiswal, 1972; Patni, 1983; Dwivedi, 1983, Pratap and Srivastava, 1984; Sawhney, 1984; Mishra 1991; Das, 1993; Nayak, 1994, Singh, 1997 and Chandrakumar and Arockiaswamy, 1997). The findings of these researches are contradictory to the results of the present one.

The overall findings with respect to high-low achiever differences indicate that high achievers have more preference for hedonistic and power values. It implies that high achievers are more pleasure seekers. They have strong desire to derive satisfaction from physical comforts and rest. They are the believers in the fulfilment of personal desires. Further they want to exercis their authority over the subordinate employees. They want to occupy higher position. They believe in ruling in a small place is better than serving in a big place. This result seems to be quite surprising because it has been generally observed that high achievers are more industrious, hard worker and painstaker than the low achievers. The present finding might have emerged because of the small number of subjects of high achievers was included in the study.

On the other hand, low achievers have strong inclination towards social and knowledge values. It implies that low achievers like to do social service and think for the development of their community. They like to help needy persons and enjoy making friendship. Besides they like to be scholars for advancing knowledge by discovering new facts and desire to study for the advancement of knowledge. However, these findings need further investigation. No parallel study is available to support or contradict the findings of the study, but some studies using different tools of values have reported the relationship between the values and achievement (Thomson, 1961; Cole and Miller, 1967; Walker, 1970; Hapner, 1970; Bellucci 1970; Makhija, 1973 and Verma and Srivastava, 1997). Rath (1994) concluded that there were significant differences of values between the high achievers and low achievers.

IMPLICATIONS

No research effort can be said to be worthwhile if it does not emanate some of the important educational implications. The area of higher secondary students' values has emerged as a new star on the horizon of educational research. In India attempts made in this direction may be counted on finger tips. As mentioned earlier the present study has been concentrating on exploring the value profiles of the students across their streams and comparing their value patterns. The study under reference has yielded several important and interesting findings and these findings may be utilised in various ways. The educational implications of the present piece of research are stated below :

1. The sample students, irrespective of their academic streams, sex and achievement level, have shown their least concern for social values. It is neither an expected nor a desirable finding. It is, therefore, for the teachers and guidance workers to find out the causes of least preference for social values among the higher secondary students. They should also suggest the remedies for developing social values among the higher secondary students.
2 In the present study, it was found that both the rural and urban higher secondary students had least preference to the health values as last but one (*i.e.* 9th rank). This indicates that the sample students are not conscious of their health practices. It is neither an expected nor a desirable findings. A further probe into the matter is, therefore, called for to investigate as to why the higher secondary students have least preference for health values.
3. It was found that in some values, science, arts and commerce students differed significantly. Since every student is expected to have values of his or her own choice, necessary guidance may help them to have proper understanding of it so that they will have desirable value patterns.

4 The values of students having rural and urban background (irrespective of their academic streams) differed to a significant level. In all the ten values, the urban students had scored significantly higher than their rural counterparts. The disparity needs to be removed by taking appropriate measures.

5. It was also found that in certain values, male and female students (as a whole) had different value preferences. For example in aesthetic, hedonistic, power, family prestige and health values male students had scored higher than the female students. On the other hand the female students had more social and economic values. It is essential on the part of the teacher to take note of it and factors responsible for it should be identified and suitable measures should be taken to improve upon the situation.

6. The findings of the present study revealed that high and low achievers (as a whole) differed significantly in their social, knowledge, hedonistic and power values. In hedonistic and power values high achievers had scored significantly higher than the low achievers while the low achievers had more social and knowledge values than the high achievers. It means that the high achievers are pleasure-seekers and power-lovers. On the contrary, the low achievers have shown their concern for the development of the community and thirst for knowledge. This findings is quite surprising. A further probe into the matter is, therefore, called for.

7. The findings of the present study may be utilized by educational planners, teachers and administrators, in order to assess the pattern of values of students and developing strategies for tonning up the educational atmosphere in the institutions.

8. The study may be of interest to teachers and heads of the institutions who wish to get feedback about their own functioning with a view to improving performance and practices.

9. The study may provide sufficient clues towards improving the organisational climate in the educational institutions.

10. The study will give an impetus to research in education and would encourage the young researchers to think in the new direction of students' values with its varied ramifications in order to contribute significantly to the body of knowledge.

SUGGESTIONS

On the basis of the findings of the study, the following suggestions are offered :

1. Further research may be conducted at the national level so that the generalization of wider nature may be made.
2. Similar study may be conducted on students of higher education covering a large number of faculties.
3. To understand the value patterns of students fully, other variables as intellectual potential, motivation, study habits cultural background, educational aspiration, socio-economic status, attitude and interest etc., may be included in further research.
4. Similar studies may be conducted by controlling the intervening variables like caste, culture, sex and socio-economic status.
5. More objective assessment of values can be made by using some other forms of tests and techniques.
6. The sample from other districts of Orissa and from large number of higher secondary schools may be taken to broadbass the study.
7. The present study can not be comprehensive and final in itself unless subjected to many variations. The sample size can be enlarged comprising of stratifications based on age, grade, caste, culture and socio-economic status.
8. The findings of the study needs to be cross-validated

BIBLIOGRAPHY

Adhikari, G.S. and Adhikari, S. (1987). "Comparative Study of Values Among Rural and Urban Students", *Bhartiya Adhunik Sikhya, 4* (4), 42-43.

Ahluwalia, S.P. and Kalia, A.K. (1984). "An Investigation into the Urban-Rural Differences in Values, Adjustment, Personality and Intelligence Scores of Adolescents", *Journal of the Institute of Educational Research,* 28 (3), 21-25.

Allport, G.W. *et al.* (1931). *Study of Values.* Boston : Houghton Mifflin Company.

Anantharaman, R.N. (1980). "The Effect of Social Class, Sex and Rural-Urban Locality on Values", *Journal of Psychological Researches,* 24 (2), 112-164.

Annama, A.K. (1984). Values, Aspirations and Adjustment of College Students in Kerala, In M.B. Buch (ED) *Fourth Survey of Research in Education* (1983-88), New Delhi : N.C.E.R.T.

Arccnaaw, C. (1990). "Personality Characteristics, Interests and Values of Differentially Achieving Ablc College Students". *Dissertation Abstract International,*52 (3), 183.

Aristotle, T. and Peters, F.H. (1898). *The Nicomachean Ethics of Aristotle.* London: Kegan Paul, Trench, Trubner and Co. Ltd.

Ayer, A.J. (1946). *Language, Truth and Logic.* London : Gollancz.

Begum, S.S. and Hafees, A. (1964). "A Study of Individual and Social Values" *Indian Journal of Psychology.* 39 (1), 35-46.

Bellucci, J.T. (1970). "The contribution of values in the predicting success in Practical Nursing Training Programme". *Dissertation Abstract International,* 31, 2731-2732A.

Bhatanagar, R.P. (1963). "A Differential Study of Values of Male Graduates", *Journal of Education and Psychology,* 21 (2), 66-73.

Bhatanagar, J.K. (1971). "A Cross Cultural Study of Values", *Psychological Studies,* 16 (1), 22-28.

Bhatanagar, I. (1984). A Study of Some Family Characteristics as Related to Secondary School Students Activism Values Adjustment and School Learning In, *M.B. Buch (ED) Fourth Survey of Research in Education* (1983-88), New Delhi, N.C.E.R.T.

Bhyrappa, S.L. (1968). *Values in Modern Indian Educational Thought.* New Delhi: N.C.E.R.T. (MIMEO).

Bhusan, A. and Ahuja, M. (1980). "Values Among High and Low Achieving M.Ed. Correspondence Students Belonging to Different Socio-Economic Level", *Quest in Education,* 17 (2), 152-164.

Bond, E.J. (1983). *Reason and Value.* London: Combridge University Press.

Broudy, H.S. (1965). *Building a Philosophy of Education.* New Delhi: Prentice-Hall of India Pvt. Ltd.

Brubacher, J.S. (1978). *Modern Philosophies of Education.* New Delhi: Tata Mc Graw Hill Publishing Co. Ltd.

Cattell, R.B. Sealy, A.P. and Sweney, A.B. (1966). "What Can Personality and Motivation Source Trait Measurement add to the Prediction of School Achievement", *British Journal of Educational Psychology,* 36, 280-295.

Chandrakumar, P.S. and Arockiaswamy, S. (1997). "Gender Difference in the Value Orientation Among the College Students", *Indian Educational Abstracts,* 2, Jannuary, 35.

Chandrakumar, P.S. and Arockiaswamy, S. (1997). "A Study of the Correlates of Value System of College Students", *Indian Educational Abstracts,* 3, July, 24.

Cole, C.W. and Miller, C.D. (1967) "Relevance of Expressed Values to Academic Performance", *Journal of Counselling & Psychology* ,14 (3), 272-276.

Das, R.S. (1990). *A Study of the Value Pattern of High School Students in Relation to Their Participation in Co-curricular Activities.* M. Phil. Dissertation, Edu. H.P.U., Shimla.

Das, C.R. (1993). *A Study of Value Profiles of Students of Science, Arts and Commerce at the Higher Secondary Level of Education,* Unpublished M.Ed. Dissertation, Berhampur University.

Daud, M. (1991). Value Differences Among College Students. Paper Presented at the 79th Session of the Indian Science Congress, Baroda.

Davidson, R.A. (1970). "A Study of the Personality Traits and Values System of High School Athletes and Non-Athletes", *Dissertation Abstract International* 30 (9,10), 3777-A.

De, B. and Jaiswal, M.P. (1972). "Sex Differences in Value Patterns of Adolescent Students", *Indian Educational Review,* 7 (1), 107-114.

Dewinter, W. (1961). "Values and Achievement in a Freshman Psychological Course", *Journal of Educational Research,* 54 (5), 183-186.

Diwedi, C.B. (1983). An Investigation into the Changing Social Values and their Educational Implications, In M.B. Buch (ED) *Fourth Survey of Research in Education* (1983-88) New Delhi: N.C.E.R.T.

Duke, W.F. (1995). "Psychological Studies of Values", *Psychological Bulletin,* 52, 24-50.

Durkheim, E. (1956). *Education and Sociology* Glencoe: Free Press-Entwistle, N.J. (1972). "Students Personality and their Academic Performance in different types of Institutions" in H.J. Butcher and Earnest Rudd (eds), *Contemparary problems in Higher Education,* New York: McGraw Hill Book Com. 59-70.

Everett, W.G. (1918). *Moral values.* New York: Holt, Rinehart and Winston, Inc.

Gajjar, J.J. (1985). *Psycho-Philosophical Perspectives of Value Oriented Education,* Paper Presented at the Inter-disciplinary Seminar on Value Oriented Education, Aligarh Muslim University.

Garrett, H.E. (1973). *Statistics in Psychology and Education.* Bombay: Vakils, Feffer and Simons Ltd.

Gaur, R.S. (1980). "Values System in the Personality of Urban and Rural Adolescents", *Journal of Indian Education,* 5 (6), 10-13.

Good, C.V. (1959). *Dictionary of Education.* New York: Mc Graw Hill Book Co. Inc., 416.

Goswami, N.S. (1983). A Study of Value Orientation of Post-Basic Schools in Gujarat, In M.B. Buch (ED) *Fourth Survey of Research in Education* (1983-88), New Delhi: N.C.E.R.T.

Government of India (1964). *Report of the Committee on Religious and Moral Instruction.* New Delhi: Ministry of Education.

Government of India (1964-66). *Report of the Indian Education Commission,* New Delhi: Ministry of Education.

Goyal, B.R. (1979). *Documents on Social Moral and Spiritual values in Education,* New Delhi: N.C.E.R.T.

Gupta, N.L. (1992). *A Search for Human Values.* New Delhi: Arya Book Depot.

Hamid, P.N. and Flay, B.R. (1974). "Changes in Locus of Control as a Function of Value Modification", *British Journal of Social and Clinical Psychology,* 13, 143-150.

Hapner, E.M. (1970). "Self-concept, Values and Needs of Maxican American Under-Achievers", *Dissertation Abstract International,* 31, 2736-A.

Harriman, P.L. (1947). *The New Distionary of Psychology.* New York: The Philosophical Library Inc., 269.

Harrick, R.W. (1978). "Values Comparision of College Students and Instructors of Selected Business Courses", *Dissertation Abstract International,* 38 (8), 4716-A.

Hiriyanna, M. (1975). *Indian Conception of Values.* Mysore: Kaayalaya Publishers.

Hollins, T.H.B. (ed). (1964). *Aims of Education: A Philosophic Approach.* Manchester: Manchester University Press.

Huntley, C.W. (1958). "Allport-Vernon study of Values (Old Form) in Indian Situations (Group Differences)". *The Indian Psychological Bulletin,* 3 (2), 46-47.

Loustein, S. (1972). "Changes in Personal and Inter Personal Values by Sex and Occupational Groups in Grades IX Through XII", *Journal of Educational Research,* 66(3), 135-141.

Kabir, H. (1964). *Indian Philosophy of Education* : Bombay: Asia Publishing House (Reprint).

Kalia, A.K. (1982). *A Study of Values and Ideals of Early Adolescents Living in Different Types of Home Environment.* Ph. D. Thesis, Edu, P.U., Chandigarh.

Kalia, A.K. And Mathur, S.S. (1985). "Value Preferences of Aadolescents Studying in Schools with Different Socio-Economic Environments", *Asian Journal of Psychology and Education,* 15 (1), 1-6.

Kalra, R.M. (1976). *Curriculum, Based on Values in a Developing Country with Special Reference to India.* Ambala Cantt: Indian Publications Bureau.

Kar, N.N. (1996). *Value Education-A Philosophical Analysis.* Ambala Cantt: The Associated Publishers.

Katiyar, P.C. (1976). A Study of Values and Vocational Preferences of the Intermediate Class Students in U.P., in, M.B. Bruch (Ed) *Second Survey of Research in Education.* 1972-77, New Delhi: N.C.E.R.T.

Kirandeep and Kansal, M.R. (1989). "Emerging Values Patterns of College Students", *Trends in Education,* 18 (1), 65-71.

Kirpal, P. (1987). "Values in Education", in *Education in India-Some Critical Issues* (Ed). C.L. Sapra and Y.P. Aggarwal. New Delhi: Sterling Publishers Pvt. Ltd., 22-28.

Kaul, G.N. (1984) *"Values and Education in Independent India.* Ambala Cantt: The Associated Publishers.

Kluckhohn, C. (1951). "Values and Value Orientation in the Theory of Action: An Exploration in Definition and Classification", In, T. Parsons and E.A. Shills (Eds), *Towards a General Theory of Social Action.* Cambridge : Harvard University Press.

Kneller, G.F. (1964). *Introduction to Philosophy of Education.* New York: John Wiley and Sons, Inc.

Kohlberg. L. (1963). "Moral Development and Identification", In *Child Psychology* (Eds) H.W. Stevenson, Chicago: University of Chicago Press.

Kohlberg, L. (1964). "Development of Moral Character and Ideology", In *Review of Child Development Research* (Ed) M.L. Hoffman and L.W. Hoffman, New York: Russel Sage.

Kholberg, L. (1969). "Stage and Sequence", In, D.A. Goslin (Ed) *Handbook of Socialization Theory and Research* Chicago: Rand McNally.

Kumar, A. (1984). "A Comparison of Study of Values of Science and Commerce Undergraduates at Different Levels of Socio-Economic Status", Indian Education Review, *19(1), 136-142.*

Kumari, K. (1981). "A Study of the Effect of Personality on Value Pattern", *Indian Psychological Review,* 20 (1) 13-17.

Kumari, K. (1981). *Personality Needs, Moral Judgement and Value Patterns of Secondary School Teachers—A Critical Analysis.* Ph.D. Thesis, Eds. Gorakhpur University.

Kundu, R. and Sanyal, N. (1984). "A value Profile of College Students", *Social Change,* 14 (1), 9-12.

Macaiver, R.M and Page, C.H. (1950). *Society : An Introductory Analysis.* London : Macmillan.

Makhija, G.K. (1973). Intraction Among Values, Interests and Intelligence and Its Impact on Scholastic Achievement, In M.B. Bush (ed), *Third Survey of Research in Education* (1978-83), New Delhi: N.C.E.R.T.

Manav, R.N. (1981). A Study on Attitudes, Self-Concept and Values of Professional and Non-professional College Students and Relationship of these Variables with their Achievement" Ph.D. Thesis, Merrut University.

Maslow, A.H. (1956). "Toward a Humanistic Psychology", *Etc.*, 13, 10-12.

Maslow, A.H. (ed) (1959). *New Knowledge in Human Values.* New York: Harper and Brothers.

Maslow, A.H. (1970). *Motivation and Personlity* (sec Ed.) New York: Harper.

Mishra, H.S. (1991). *A Study of Certain Sociological Background Variables of Values in High Schools Students,* Unpublished M.Ed. Dissertation, Berhampur University.

Mohanty, M. (1996). "Values Pattern and Locus of Control of Postgraduates Female Students and their Family Background", *University News,* 34 (3) 11-16.

Moore, G.S. (1903). *Principia Ethica.* London: Cambridge University Press.

Morris, C. (1957). *Varieties in Human values.* Chicago: The University of Chicago Press.

Mouly, G.J. (1964). *The Science of Educational Research.* New Delhi: Eurasia Publishing House Pvt. Ltd.

Mukherjee, R.K. (1969). *Social Structure of Values.* Delhi: S.Chand Pub. Co.

Mulder, C.T. (1974). "A Study of Parents, Students and Teacher Value Systems in a Mid-West Christian School System", *Disseratation Abstract International,* 34 (7).

Narayanan, S. *et. al.* (1994). "Values Orientation Among Indian College Students", *Journal of Psychological Researches,* 38 (3), 42-51.

Nayak, A.C. (1994). *A Study of Value-Variations in the Ninth and Twelfth Grade Students,* Unpublished M.Ed. Dissertation, Berhampur University.

Nazarethrjm, M.P. and Waples, M.E. (1980). *To Live or not to Live with Values.* New Delhi: All India Association of Catholic Schools.

Ojha, R.K. (1984). *Study of Values.* Agra: National Psychological Corporation.

Pal. S.K. (1967). "Values of Students in Four Professions Under Indian Conditions", *Journal of Social Psychology* 77, 297-298.

Parmar, M.S. (1986). Sociological Study of Social Values and Aspirations of Students of Colleges of Rural Backgrounds, In M.B. Buch (ed) *Fourth Survey of Research in Education* (1983-88) New Delhi, N.C.E.R.T.

Passi, B.K. and Singh, P. (1991). *Value Education.* Agra: Bhargava Book House.

Gupta, S.N. (1978). *The Indian Concept of Values,* New Delhi: Monohar Pubs.

Patel, M.G. (1981). A Study of the Prevalent Value System of the Students of South Gujarat Studying in the Standard X and XI, In M.B. Buch (ed) *Fourth Survey of Research in Education,* (1983-88) New Delhi, N.C.E.R.T.

Patni, U. (1983). The Values held by College Girls and their Relation with Achievement Motivation, In M.B. Buch (ed) *Fourth Survey of Research in Education,* (1983-88) New Delhi, N.C.E.R.T

Paul, P.V. (1986). A Study of Value Orientations M.B. Buch (ed) of Adolescent Boys and Girls, In M.B. Buch (ed) *Fourth Survey of Research in Education,* (1983-88) New Delhi, N.C.E.R.T.

Peck, R,F. and Havinghurst, R.J. (1960). *The Psychology of Character* Development, New york: Wiley.

Perry, R.B. (1950). *General Theory of Value* Cambridge Mass: Harvard University Press.

Perry, R.B.(1954). *The Realms of Value.* Cambridge Mass: Harvard University Press.

Peters, R.S. (1981). *Moral Development and Moral Education.* London: George Allen and Unwin Co.

Piaget, J. (1948) *The Moral Development of the Child.* New York: Free Press.

Piaget, J. (1960). *The Moral Judgement of the Child.* Translated by M. Gabain, New York : Free Press.

Prakash, V. (1994). *A Study of Educational Aspirations, School Adjustment and Values of +2 Arts and Science Male Students in Relation to School Environment.* Unpublished Ph.D. thesis (ed), Punjabi University.

Pratap, S. and Srinivastava, S.K. (1984). "A Study of Sex Differences Among College Going Students towards Different Types of Values", *Journal of the Institution of Educational Research* 8 (1), 11-13.

Radhakrishnan, S. (1931). *The Hindu view of Life.* London : George Allen and Unwin Ltd.

Radhakrishnan, S. (1947). *An Ideallistic View of Life.* London : George Allen and Unwin Ltd.

Radhakrishnan, S. (1956). *Indian Philosophy* (vol. I and vol. II). London: George Allen and Unwin Ltd.

Rajput, B.M. (1985). Academic Achievement as a Function of Some Personality Variables and Socio-economic Factors In M.B. Buch (ed) *Fourth Survey of Research in Education* (1983-88), New Delhi: N.C.E.R.T

Ramji, M.T (1973). *Value-oriented School Education.* New Delhi: N.C.E.R.T

Raths, L. *et. al.* (1978). *Values and Teaching: Working With Values in the Class-room,* Ohio: Charies. Merrill.

Rath, V. (1994). A Study of Attitudes and Values on Achievement of IX Grade Boys Unpublished. M.Ed. Dissertation, Berhampur University.

Reddy, V.N.K. (1979). *Man, Education and Values* Delhi: B.R. Pub.

Reddy, N.Y. (1980). *Values and Attitudes of Indian Youth.* New Delhi: Light and Life Publications.

Rizvi, S.A.H. (1986). A Study of Attitudes towards Religious Education in Relation to Certain Value Orientations, In M.B. Buch (ed), *Fourth Survey of Research in Education* (1983-88) New Delhi: N.C.E.R.T.

Rokeach, M. (1973). *The Nature of Human Values.* New York: Free Press.

Russell, B. (1940). *An Inquiry into Meaning and Truth,* London : George Allen and Unwin Ltd.

Ruhela, S.P.(ed) (1990). *Human Values and Education,* New Delhi : Sterling Publishers Pvt. Ltd.

Sahgal, K. (1980). Co-education and Non-co-educational System as Related with Personality Traits, Self-concept and Values of Women Students, In M.B. Buch (ed) *Third Survey of Research in Education* (1978-83) New Delhi: N.C.E.R.T.

Sahney, S.P. (1984). A Comparative Study of Personality, Adjustment and Values of Delinquents and Non-Delinquents, In M.B. Buch (ed) *Fourth Survey of Research in Education* (1983-88) New Delhi: N.C.E.R.T.

Sanyal, N. (1991). "A Value Profile of Male Science Students of Calcutta University", *Indian Journal of Applied Psychology,* 28 (1) 24-29.

Saxena, G. (1972). Social Background, Values and Aspirations of Students in an Indian Town, In M.B. Buch (ed) *Third Survey of Research in Education* (1978-83) New Delhi: N.C.E.R.T. Sawhney, K.K. (1984). A Factorial Study of the Value System of Educated Youth in an Indian Locale, In M.B. Buch (ed) *Fourth Survey of Research in Education* (1983-88) New Delhi: N.C.E.R.T.

Sathadri, C. *et.al.* (ed) (1992). *Education in Values—A Source Book,* New Delhi: N.C.E.R.T.

Sharma, D.D. (1977). Differential Values of Students and Teachers-As a Function of Various Social Factors, In M.B. Buch (ed) *Third Survey of Research in Education* (1978-83) New Delhi: N.C.E.R.T.

Sherman, G.G. (1971). "An Investigation of Inter Personal Values of Negro and White Junior College Students", *Sociology of Education,* 44, 356-360.

Sherry, G.P. and Verma, R.P. (1978). *Manual for Personal Values Questionnaire* Agra: National Psychological Corporation.

Shinn, R.L. (1979) "Education in Values Acculturation and Exploration", *Teachers College Record,* 80, (3).

Simon, S.B. and Krischebaum, L. (1973). *Readings in Values Clarification.* Minneapolis, Minn: Winston press.

Singh, S.P. (1986). Harijan Students: Their Values, Problems and Level of Frustration, In M.B. Buch (ed) *Fourth Survey of Research in Education.* (1983-88) New Delhi: N.C.E.R.T.

Singh, R.K. *et. al.* (1990). "A Study of Value System of Tribal Students of Chotanagpur in their Christian and Non-Christian Tribal Social Background," *Indian Psychological Review,* 35 (12). 26-33.

Singh, R.P. (1997). "A Study of Values of Urban and Rural Adolescent Students", *Indian Educational Abstracts,* 2, January, 38.

Smith, P.G. (ed). (1970). *Theories of Value and Problems of Education.* University of Illinois Press: Board of Trustees of the University of Illinois.

Soble, R.K. (1978). "Student Value Change and Congruency with Faculty Values in Professional Education Related to Reference Group Theory", *Dissertation Abstract International,* 37 (11) 7346-4.

Solan, D. (1979). "Education and Value", Editorial *Teachers College Record,* 80 (3), February.

Srivastava, A.B.L. and Bhatkulikar, S.C. (1980). Sampling Techniques for Educational Surveys, Paper presented in Training Course in Sample Survey Methods in Education, R.C.E., Bhopal, Ct.

Srivastava, S.S. (1982). 'Problems, Aspirations' Values and Personality Patterns of Tribal Students of Mirzapur, In M.B. Buch (ed) *Third Survey of Research in Education* (1978-83) New Delhi: N.C.E.R.T.

Srivastave, S.K. (1997) "Values in Relation to Personality Triats and Self-concept *Indian Educational Abstracts* 3, July. 37"

Stevenson, C.L. (1994). *Ethics and Language.* New Haven, Connecticut: Yale University Press.

Tewari, R.K. and Tewari, R (1997). "Values Among College Students: Caste Differences", *Indian Educational Abstracts,* 3 July, 37.

Thomas, T.M. (1970). Indian Educational Reforms in Cultural Perspective, Delhi: S. Chand & Co.

Thomas, O.E. (1961). "High School Students Values Emergent or Traditional". *California Journal of Educational Research,* 12. 132-146.

Tiwari, G and Singh, R. (1973). "Value Pattern as a Function of Sex", *Indian Journal of Psychology and Education* 31, 152-160.

Upamaneyu, I. (1989). *Values Pattern of Students Studying in a Missionery School, DAV School and Senior Secondary School of Salon Town of H.P.: A Comparative Study.* M.Ed. Dissertation, H.P. University Shimla.

Verma, M. (1986). *Study of Values.* Agra : National Psychological Corporation.

Verma, B.P. and Kali Ram (1988). "A Study of the Values of Adolescents of Average Socio-Economic Status in Relation to Urban-Rural Background", *Journal of the Institute of Educational Research,* 12 (3), 21-24.

Verma, B.P. *et. al.* (1993). "Values of Adolescent Students as a Function of their Sex and Rural-Urban Inhabitation", *Indian Educational Review,* XXVIII, 1, 71-79.

Verma, B.P. *et.al.* (1998). "A Study of Personal Values of SCS and Non-SCS Students", *Indian Educational Abstracts,* 4, January, 76.

Verma, D. (1996). "A Study of Values Pattern Among College Youth of Rohilkhand Region with Special Reference to Sense of Responsibility", *Indian Educational Abstracts,* 1, July, 40.

Verma, D.P. and Srivastava, S.S. (1997). "Academic Achivement and Value Pattern of the Best Athletes of Vidya Bharati", *Indian Journal of Educational Research,* 16 (1), 47-54.

Verma, M. (1966). *An Introduction to Educational and Psychological Research.* Bombay: Asia Publishing House, 51.

Vivekananda, S. (1932). *The Complete Works of Swami Vivekananda,* Part IV, Almora, Mayavati: Advaita Ashram.

Walker, H.E. (1970) "A Study of Differences in Expressed values of High School Seniors of Selected Secondary Schools", *Dissertation Abstract International,* 31, 2200-A.

Wartz, P. *et.al.* (1962). "Value Variations in the Fourth and Sixth Grade Students", *Journal of Educational Research,* 56 (2) 96-99.

Winter, W. (1962). "Student Values and Grades in General Psychology", *Journal of Educational Research,* 55(7), 331-333.

Wolman, B.B. (1973). *Dictionary of Behavioural Science,* New York: Yan Nastrand Reinhold Co., 291.

Zaidi, S. (1985). *A Plea for Value Oriented Education,* Key Note Adress to Interdisciplinary Seminar on Value Oriented Education at AMU. Feb. Zamen, G.S.

(1982). A Study of Social, Religious and Moral Values of Students of Class XI and their Relationship with Moral Character Traits and Personility Adjustment, In M.B. Buch (ed) *Fourth Survey of Research in Education* (1983-88) New Delhi: N.C.E.R.T.

■■■■

Index